theopentable
an invitation to know God

the opentable
an invitation to know God
participant's guide

by Donald **Miller**
with John **MacMurray**

THOMAS NELSON
Since 1798

NASHVILLE   DALLAS   MEXICO CITY   RIO DE JANEIRO   BEIJING

Published in Nashville, Tennessee, by Thomas Nelson. Thomas Nelson is a registered trademark of Thomas Nelson, Inc.

Thomas Nelson, Inc. titles may be purchased in bulk for educational, business, fund-raising, or sales promotional use. For information, please e-mail SpecialMarkets@ThomasNelson.com.

Unless otherwise noted, Scripture quotations are from THE NEW KING JAMES VERSION. © 1982 by Thomas Nelson, Inc. Used by permission. All rights reserved.

Scripture quotations noted MSG are from The Message by Eugene H. Peterson. © 1993, 1994, 1995, 1996, 2000. Used by permission of NavPress Publishing Group. All rights reserved.

Scripture quotations noted NCV are from the New Century Version®. © 2005 by Thomas Nelson, Inc. Used by permission. All rights reserved.

Scripture quotations noted NIV are from the HOLY BIBLE: NEW INTERNATIONAL VERSION®. Copyright © 1973, 1978, 1984 by International Bible Society. Used by permission of Zondervan Publishing House. All rights reserved.

Published in association with Alive Communications.

The publishers are grateful to Kate Etue for her collaboration and writing assistance in developing the content for this book.

ISBN: 978-1-4185-1095-4

Printed in the United States of America
09 10 11 12 RRD 5 4 3

Contents

The operating manual for life on earth is sadly neglected. We don't really need a Bible for Dummies, *since the meaning of the inspired Word of God is clear enough to meet your needs. The Scriptures are full of interesting, shocking, helpful and inspiring stories—but unfortunately, they go unexplored by many of us.*

—Former President Jimmy Carter, recipient of the Nobel Prize for Peace

Introduction

The fact I believe in God is as perplexing to me as it must be for somebody who does not believe. In ways, believing in God has felt as strange as a belief in aliens, and I think more than a few people perceive a belief in God to be as odd. And yet I believe. I believe even though there is little I can do to prove God. I have never sat in a room with God and talked to him face-to-face or met him on the street. I've not had an e-mail correspondence with God, although I'd like to. I have no real proof God exists, at least not the kind of scientific proof most scientists want. And yet, as I said, I believe. And I don't believe in aliens or the tooth fairy or Santa Claus. My belief in God is something very different. I somehow know he exists, and yet I don't know how I know.

I liken the experience to falling in love, in a way. Love is not something I can prove, and yet I experience love, and the feeling and concept manifest itself in very real action. Many of us navigate our lives around the supposed existence of love. We are loyal to friends, are romantic with partners, marry, have and love children, and yet no scientist can quantifiably prove love. My knowledge of God is not unlike this concept of love. And by that I do not mean to say I have romantic feelings for God—only that my hope and desire for a being greater than myself is aimed at something that, to me, has responded with an affirmation that he is there and is somehow interacting with me. This knowing I am talking about is based on propositions made by Jesus, and found in the Bible.

While many rational arguments have been made regarding the existence of God, and Scripture itself often appeals to our better logic, I am still aware of how unsophisticated this belief sounds to the average hearer. Even the apostle Paul, one of the writers who contributed to the Bible, said a belief in God will sound like foolishness to those who haven't experienced him (1 Corinthians 1:18). For some of you, hearing somebody say they believe in God causes you to roll your eyes. It sounds

like foolishness precisely because a belief in God sounds like a belief in myth or magic. And yet I don't consider myself a foolish person. And so I am stuck. I believe in a God I cannot see, and in ways I cannot prove, and yet my belief goes on all the same. After a long time battling it, I have decided to simply give in to what I cannot deny, and so sound foolish. I can no more separate myself from a belief in God than I can separate myself from a belief in love. There are some realities we all agree on that simply cannot be proved through the limited resources available to a human being.

And yet I sympathize with the struggle of the agnostic. Last week I sat with a woman in a hallway at a large political convention in Denver. It was her job to usher speakers in and out of a rehearsal room. I was at the convention to deliver a closing prayer. We were waiting outside when she asked about my faith, about how I came to believe. I told her it was a mystery, not unlike how I came to realize love or beauty. She looked at me very seriously and told me she always wanted to believe, that she saw her friends who believe and she envied their faith. She said if she believed, her life would have a safety net and she would have a guide. Her eyes were tender and she had a longing disposition as she told me these things. I didn't know what to tell her, except to say if she prayed and asked God to help her believe, perhaps he would. I don't know if that is true, to be honest, but I hope it is. And I hope she encounters God in the same way I have.

As unsophisticated as it sounds to believe in God, I do not know if I could operate without this belief. I am not one of the bold ones who can look into the dark passage of my future, the brevity of my time, and celebrate, as some do, the meaninglessness of it all. I need a God to help me understand life and love, and that sunsets and sunrises, death and birth are all happening for a reason. My faith in God does this for me.

That said, I am not exactly sure how to introduce somebody to God. I do not believe the Catholics have everything figured out, or the Baptists or the Buddhists. I believe all religious systems are touched by man and therefore tarnished. What I am saying is I think the religious institution through which you were probably given this book is imperfect and therefore, at least in some way, dilutes the goodness and pureness of God. And so to introduce somebody to God through the worldly methodology of religion is to do a disservice. I would think the only way a person could make their way through the religious landscape is to have a great deal of forgiveness for those who traffic there.

That said, we will focus little on religious tradition, and much on the person of Jesus as he is presented in Scripture. The point of the Bible, in many ways, is to reveal Jesus as the Son of God, and as God himself. If you like, you can view this book as a series of exchanges between yourself and Jesus, and we want you to feel the freedom to decide, for yourself, who you think he was and is. To be sure, we believe Jesus is God, and so we are biased. And the writers of Scripture believed he was God, and so are biased as well. And yet we, and the writers of Scripture, have nothing to gain from you encountering Jesus through this text. We aren't keeping tabs of converts. This journey is truly between you and God.

What we want to do in this book is move out of the way as much as possible and point you toward God as he explains himself in the Bible. You can think of these daily readings as encounters with God in which you develop an idea of him, not too different from a series of blind dates. If, in spending time with him, you come to a kind of faith, then I think this book will have served its purpose. If not, I hope there will be another time in which you will see what it is we have come to see—that God is there, and he is good, and he is trying to interact with you.

We call this book *The Open Table* because many who read through it will do so in a small group of people who have agreed they can talk about anything without being judged. I believe in a God who takes us as we are and asks that I do the same. I

think the only rule is honesty and consideration of other people's ideas and experiences.

If you are going through this book alone, it may help to keep a journal and ask questions of God or make observations or comments in the form of a prayer.

I hope you come to know him in the way we have come to know him. And I affirm your willingness and desire to take that question that exists in your soul and seek resolution. May God bless and keep you on this journey.

Sincerely,
Donald Miller

What Do You Think of When You Think about God?

Opening Thoughts

- When you were young, how did you imagine God?

- What is your personal history with the church? You may want to write a paragraph or two describing your experiences.

- Do you believe God likes you?

■ Day 1: Can I Be Myself Around God?

I grew up in a small church down south. It had *rules*. We dressed up on Sunday, we did not use profanity, and we did *not* drink or dance. But none of this was any fun, to be honest. And so I adapted; I learned to have a dual personality. At church, I knew how to dress and how to act, but when I was away, I drank and cussed and even danced a bit (though I don't think anybody else would have called it dancing). Regardless, from an early age, my religious life was separate from the rest of my life. I thought there was a Jesus side of life and then a regular side of life, and while I believed "theologically" that God made the earth and everything in it, I lived as though he only made the church and had a fondness for steeples, hymnals, and

melodramatic preachers, but was largely unfamiliar with hip-hop music.

What I never realized, however, was that the Jesus whom we claimed to follow didn't separate his spiritual life from his regular life at all. The Jesus in Scripture, in fact, looks very little like the average American Christian.

In the Gospel of John, one of four brief biographies written about Christ in the Bible, the writer (John) tells a story about Jesus being invited to a wedding:

> On the third day there was a wedding in Cana of Galilee, and the mother of Jesus was there. Now both Jesus and His disciples were invited to the wedding. And when they ran out of wine, the mother of Jesus said to Him, "They have no wine."
>
> Jesus said to her, "Woman, what does your concern have to do with Me? My hour has not yet come."
>
> His mother said to the servants, "Whatever He says to you, do it."
>
> Now there were set there six waterpots of stone, according to the manner of purification of the Jews, containing twenty or thirty gallons apiece. Jesus said to them, "Fill the waterpots with water." And they filled them up to the brim. And He said to them, "Draw some out now, and take it to the master of the feast." And they took it. When the master of the feast had tasted the water that was made wine, and did not know where it came from (but the servants who had drawn the water knew), the master of the feast called the bridegroom. And he said to him, "Every man at the beginning sets out the good wine, and when the guests have well drunk, then the inferior. You have kept the good wine until now!"
>
> This beginning of signs Jesus did in Cana of Galilee, and manifested His glory; and His disciples believed in Him. (John 2:1–11)

As far as we know, Jesus' presence at the wedding wasn't required. Jesus was a rabbi, a kind of local Jewish pastor, yet he was there because of an invitation, not an obligation. They *wanted* him there. If you've ever planned a wedding, you know how timidly you invite a person you think is going to be a downer. You want upbeat, fun, positive people to celebrate with you, and you try to keep the downers out. Jesus wasn't a family member they had to invite; the folks who threw this wedding wanted him there, which tells us a great deal about his personality.

People liked Jesus. So, even though Jesus was a respected religious leader, they felt "at home" with him. And John makes it obvious why. He tells us Jesus *participates* in the party. He doesn't stand off to the side in a suit subtly judging people who are drinking and dancing. Quite the opposite. When the party runs out of wine, Jesus creates new wine from water right there on the spot so the party can keep going. (He doesn't say, "I'm glad you're finally done with the alcohol. Don't you know it's against our religion to drink?") Importantly, John lets us know it is the best wine they've had all night, as though to explain the thoughtfulness Jesus had toward the bride and groom and other guests. No wonder they wanted him at the wedding.

And to add to this, Jesus doesn't take credit for the miracle. Instead, he stands silently by, allowing the bridegroom to accept the congratulations. Jesus' disciples and the servants who drew the water must have been shocked that he didn't desire recognition. What kind of impression did this make on them? John wrote that they saw and witnessed Jesus' *glory*—not just in an act of creation that revealed his deity, but also in an act of kindness, pleasure, and grace that revealed his character. His acceptance of his friends moved him to be generous. His generosity was not motivated by the potential for praise or affirmation.

As we start on this study, letting go of our preconceived ideas about Jesus will be difficult. Even though I consider myself somebody who believes Jesus is the Son of God, it's still hard for me to believe he likes me and accepts me. But when I

read this passage, it helps. I think somebody who is invited to a wedding, actually makes wine so the party doesn't die down, and then refuses to take credit for the gift is a fairly likeable person who isn't going around pointing fingers at people. The Jesus of Scripture is definitely different from the Jesus most of us think about when we hear his name. The Jesus we often see represented on television can sometimes be angry, judgmental, and *morally superior.* He certainly doesn't seem like the kind of guy who could hang out with the average person. And yet the Jesus of Scripture is different. He liked people, and apparently he liked for people to be happy.

And that leads me to believe this guy might like me. And I think he might like you too.

As a result of this event, John tells us that he (and the other disciples) trusted this man, Jesus. And I think John wrote this for another reason too. I think he put this story in his biography because he wanted you and me to know Jesus is trustworthy; that if we want to, we can sit and talk to him and be honest. And he will listen. And he will not make us feel inferior for having shared our true selves with him.

Closing Thoughts

If you could have a conversation with Jesus, what would you want to talk about? What would you tell him? What questions would you ask?

■ Day 2: Does God Know about Me?

One of the more important ideas proposed by Christians is that Jesus, who claimed to be God, actually came and lived among us. A favorite author of mine, Eugene Peterson, translated the part of the Bible that talked about Jesus being born: "The Word became flesh and blood, and moved into the neighborhood" (John 1:14 MSG). I like that take on it, to be honest. I like the idea of God having lived among us because, if we are honest, we sometimes feel God is very distant, living in a gated community somewhere north of quantum physics.

But Scripture claims God came to earth. He moved into the neighborhood, if you will. And if this is true, and the Jesus of Scripture is truly God, we can be comforted in that God is compassionate and kind. The Bible says that while Jesus was here he healed the sick and stood up against the corrupted systems that oppressed people. His very presence on earth said something significant about God. It said God gets involved. He goes all the way. Jesus took on human skin and bones and entered into our world in order to make things better for us.

All this sounds like I am talking about a traditional king or a guy running for president, but the truth is, Jesus looked nothing like that. Jesus was born into scandal, in fact. His mother was a virgin, Scripture says, becoming pregnant through the Spirit of God. Getting pregnant so young is probably frightening enough, but getting pregnant without having sex must have been mind numbing. She was engaged to a guy named Joseph, and when she became pregnant, people talked. God even went to Joseph in a dream and told him to not freak out, to be faithful to Mary and to trust. And to make matters worse, they had to travel to Bethlehem during the end of her pregnancy because the government was doing a census. When they arrived, and Mary was about to give birth, they had to stay in a barn because all the hotels were full. Scripture said that when Mary gave birth, she put Jesus into a manger, a trough that holds hay for animals. You'd think the King of the world, the Creator of all things and the Savior of all humanity would be born in a palace and revealed to the masses in a golden crib, but that isn't what happened. The Bible, the very book that is trying to convince us that Jesus is God, speaks candidly about the fact that Jesus was born into poverty, to a sweet and obedient mother and an earthly father who was nothing more than a common laborer. All that to say, if Jesus is God, then God has no fear of common men and women.

When Scripture says that God became one of us, it really means *one of us.* If Jesus is who the Scriptures say he is, one truth is undeniable about God: he has not abandoned the human race. He got involved with us by becoming one of us (see John 1:1–14). As Jesus grew, his parents noticed that he was different. He was on a mission, it seemed. He saw the world very differently from the way you and I see the world. He proclaimed grand, counterintuitive ideas as truth. And he wanted the world to know something.

Look at this description the writer Matthew gives of Jesus:

Then Jesus went about all the cities and villages, teaching
in their synagogues, preaching the gospel of the kingdom,
and healing every sickness and every disease among the
people. But when He saw the multitudes, He was moved with
compassion for them, because they were weary and scattered,
like sheep having no shepherd. (Matthew 9:35–36)

Usually, if the president comes through town, he only
spends a little bit of time with the poor and the marginalized.
Just enough time for reporters to take some photos, in fact. But
Jesus went everywhere—to all people, regardless of religious or
economic status. He wasn't trying to get votes. And while he was
with them, he taught them the truth about their infinite value;
and he taught them about his kingdom, where justice would be
accomplished.

And notice what Matthew says about Jesus' personality. He
writes that when Jesus saw the large crowds following him, "He
was moved with compassion." Matthew wants us to know that
Jesus actually cared about the people he interacted with. He
cared for them individually. And so all this begs the question:
could he care about you and me too?

That question must have been on the minds of the people
Jesus talked to. As he taught and proclaimed himself as God,
he intuitively knew many people were wondering whether or not
God even liked them. And Jesus boldly and straightly answered
their question with authority:

"Look at the birds of the air, for they neither sow nor reap nor
gather into barns; yet your heavenly Father feeds them. *Are you
not of more value than they?* . . .

"Consider the lilies of the field, how they grow: they neither
toil nor spin . . . Now if God so clothes the grass of the field, **which
today is,** and tomorrow is thrown into the oven, will He not much
more clothe you?" (Matthew 6:26–30, emphasis mine)

If we believe Jesus said these things, then it is my belief we can trust God with his creation.

Jesus' words bear repeating: If God cares for the birds and the grass and flowers, will he not care for you? Does he not consider you more important than birds, grass, and flowers?

One of the things that is most appealing to me about a relationship with Christ is that this man who claimed to be God had a love for the people he created. Whatever you've sensed from religious people or felt in the midst of your doubt and pain, know this for certain: Jesus really does care about you. No joke, no fake promise. He really does. He gave his life to show it.

Closing Thoughts

Do you believe Jesus cares for you? Why or why not?

■ Day 3: Is God Judging Me?

Early in 2008 I went to Uganda with the American Consul. While there, we met with honorable justices of the Supreme Court as well as members of Parliament. We also visited a remand home where children were being held awaiting trial. Because of the recent conflict in Northern Uganda, the courts were backed up and many of the children had been waiting in the home for a year or more. Essentially, they were being imprisoned, some for very small offenses, well past the sentence even a guilty plea might require.

The trip gave me a clearer understanding of the importance of justice. Without justice, without fair judges and an honest legal system, a society cannot succeed. My friend Bob Goff, the American Consul, was instrumental in returning the court system to Northern Uganda after the war had ended; and partly through his efforts, relative peace was reestablished in that troubled region. Justice, at least to some degree, stabilized the society and allowed people to live in more freedom.

The idea of justice is an incredibly important theme throughout the Scriptures. Early in Israel's history, God established a judicial system for the people as a way of blessing them—without it, chaos would have run rampant through their culture. In Scripture, God identifies himself as a fair judge, and later in history Jesus also is concerned with justice and setting things right in the world.

But why are we talking about this now? As someone who is new to the whole idea of having a relationship with Jesus, you're probably not too excited to focus on the idea of God as a judge. Just yesterday we were exploring the idea of whether or not Jesus even likes us, and now we're facing judgment. Isn't that the part of religion that we hate—the overbearing preacher on TV making people feel awful about their flaws, their opinions, and their desires? But this is not the type of judge Jesus seems to be. In fact, he tells us to pull the log out of our eye before we go around pointing out the speck that is in our neighbor's eye. I don't think Jesus has a lot in common with the angry preacher on TV.

But Jesus does judge, and he thinks justice is important. What is different about Jesus is that he judges rightly. He sees through the deceptive methods people use to distort justice, and he deals out responsibility and judgment accurately. Let's look at how this can bring comfort and security to us.

In John 8:1–11, a group of high-and-mighty Jews brings to Jesus a woman who had been caught in adultery, expecting him to punish her for her sins. But instead we see how tenderly,

sternly, and rightly Jesus deals with *all* parties involved. And in watching Jesus, we also get a better understanding of how he rightly judges us.

But Jesus went to the Mount of Olives.

Now early in the morning He came again into the temple, and all the people came to Him; and He sat down and taught them. Then the scribes and Pharisees brought to Him a woman caught in adultery. And when they had set her in the midst, they said to Him, "Teacher, this woman was caught in adultery, in the very act. Now Moses, in the law, commanded us that such should be stoned. But what do you say?" This they said, testing Him, that they might have something of which to accuse Him. But Jesus stooped down and wrote on the ground with His finger, as though He did not hear.

So when they continued asking Him, He raised Himself up and said to them, "He who is without sin among you, let him throw a stone at her first." And again He stooped down and wrote on the ground. Then those who heard it, being convicted by their conscience, went out one by one, beginning with the oldest even to the last. And Jesus was left alone, and the woman standing in the midst. When Jesus had raised Himself up and saw no one but the woman, He said to her, "Woman, where are those accusers of yours? Has no one condemned you?"

She said, "No one, Lord."

And Jesus said to her, "Neither do I condemn you; go and sin no more."

This is a difficult subject. God does judge. And he has the right to. He is the one who created human beings, so he is the one who has been offended when we fall short of his standard for us. Yet, Jesus' *attitude* toward this woman, who is clearly violating God's law (therefore, offending God), is not condemnatory. He is gracious and forgiving. However, he identifies her behavior as sin and tells her very straightly to not return to it.

What is interesting in this passage is that Jesus seems to see right through the schemes of the accusers. He sees that these people are comparing themselves to this woman as a way of feeling superior. And yet Jesus points out they have all sinned. (Some scholars wonder if her accusers hadn't slept with her themselves.) Jesus seems to be saying, "You guys don't get it. Everything is corrupt; nothing is what it should be; you nitpick at each other about small things when the bigger problem is that you are all severely broken." Jesus points to a problem that is in the very heart of man, and when the accusers identify with his harsh words, they drop their stones and walk away.

What is, perhaps, most beautiful about this passage is that we see the goodness of God in contrast to the depravity of man. Sinless Jesus is the only one who could see things accurately and judge with authority-issued forgiveness and warning. The picture reminds me of a mother whose kids come to her to help decide an argument, and the mother just rolls her eyes knowing both parties are guilty, but then warns and counsels them in the way of wisdom for their own benefit and maturity.

What made John remember this moment when he wrote his biography decades after Jesus' departure from earth? Was it the fact that this rabbi, who had been given the opportunity to yield a sword in authority, chose to teach and show mercy?

Through Jesus, we see God is not vindictive. His attitude is one of compassion, understanding, truth, and acceptance. He gives the adulterous woman another chance. He gives her space to grow. He does not ignore her sin, but he understands her struggle and guides her toward a mature and blessed way of living.

Is God judging me? I think John would answer that question with a yes. But he takes care to tell us that Jesus judges accurately, and his motivation is *our benefit*, not unlike a loving parent. And while we may want our parents to leave us alone

sometimes, what we are actually longing for is for somebody to guide us in love and in truth. While we may shirk away from the idea of being judged, I think we would have to agree that a world, or a life, without justice would certainly be depraved and dark.

Here's the rub. Scripture says that one day Jesus *will* judge the world. Those who have clung to their own self-righteousness (instead of Jesus' righteousness) will be held accountable and found condemned (see Matthew 25). But this story shows us that God is the God of second chances (and third, fourth, fifth, and so on). He is a God who wants to redeem, and judgment comes only if we reject his grace and choose our own corrupt system of justice instead.

Closing Thoughts

How have you judged other people? Do you think you are an honest judge of yourself? Are you too hard on yourself or too easy on yourself? Do you feel like you need an accurate judge in your life?

■ Day 4: Does God Like Me?

I have heard all my life that God loves me, and to some degree I find that easy to believe. He's God, after all—shouldn't he love everybody? But it hasn't been that easy to believe God *likes* me. And liking somebody is different from loving them. Loving people, in a general sense, almost feels like a moral obligation. Liking people is more compulsive. Liking somebody means you want to be around them and enjoy their company, and so I've wondered if the God of the universe would joke around with me at a party or want to come over to my house to watch *Monday Night Football.*

I blame some of my doubt on insecurity. People who assume others don't like them (like me in this situation) are generally a bit apprehensive, and I am sure we all have some of that in us. A good friend and my cowriter on this book, John MacMurray, showed me some passages in Scripture that convinced me Jesus was nobody to be insecure around and that Jesus actually liked most people.

In Luke 15:1 the author talks about the people who enjoyed listening to Jesus teach, and many of them, according to Luke, were tax collectors and sinners, some of the most reviled people in that culture. And yet these people didn't feel the least bit worried about approaching and having conversations with Jesus.

Jesus spent so much time with these people that religious leaders began gossiping about him. In that same passage in Luke, the Bible says the Pharisees muttered, "This Man receives sinners and eats with them" (v. 2).

Jesus didn't care whether or not his reputation was tarnished. He knew that the judgment of mere humans had no authority. Instead, he cared about people. He even seemed to enjoy and like people. At least he liked authentic people who came to him honestly. The Pharisees even noted that Jesus' relationship with these *sinners* went beyond that of a teacher or leader. They said: "The Son of Man came eating and drinking, and you say, 'Here is a glutton and a drunkard, a friend of tax collectors and "sinners"'" (Luke 7:34 NIV).

The key word in that last sentence is *friend.* Something in Jesus' actions was endearing them to him as a friend. Jesus was actually a friend of sinners. It made me wonder if Jesus would have had a cell phone, whether or not he'd be texting them all the time.

Another interesting story is the one of the rich, arrogant man who approached Jesus. Read Mark 10:17–22:

> Now as He was going out on the road, one came running, knelt before Him, and asked Him, "Good Teacher, what shall I do that I may inherit eternal life?"
>
> So Jesus said to him, "Why do you call Me good? No one is good but one, that is, God. You know the commandments: 'Do not commit adultery,' 'Do not murder,' 'Do not steal,' 'Do not bear false witness,' 'Do not defraud,' 'Honor your father and your mother.'"
>
> And he answered and said to Him, "Teacher, all these things I have kept from my youth."
>
> Then Jesus, looking at him, loved him, and said to him, "One thing you lack: Go your way, sell whatever you have and give to the poor, and you will have treasure in heaven; and come, take up the cross, and follow Me."
>
> But he was sad at this word, and went away sorrowful, for he had great possessions.

What struck me about this passage of Scripture was that even though the man was arrogant and condescending in some ways, Jesus looked at him and *loved* him. I thought that was striking, to be honest. If you ask me, when somebody is cocky and arrogant, I just want to punch him in the face. I certainly don't feel love for him.

And that made me think: if Jesus liked these people, who were serious criminals and jerks, just as much as he liked his fisherman friends and the prostitutes he interacted with, then he probably likes me too. And to be sure, there really isn't a reason to be timid or shy around him. I can let myself be known, I would guess.

Jesus liked and hung out with the marginalized, the poor, the beggars, the crippled, and the lonely who had no friends. And he also loved the rich, the self-righteous, and the arrogant.

The Gospel writers are clear on this point. Jesus didn't show favoritism. He liked everyone, even those who rejected him.

Jesus lists no criteria for us to be his friends. He doesn't need us in the way we need approval from each other. He just likes us.

Closing Thoughts

What parts of yourself or your story do you think Jesus might not like? Do these stories from the Bible help you see Jesus differently?

■ Day 5: Does God Want a Relationship with Me?

To be honest, I think I already knew God wanted to have a relationship with me. The question I've always had to face is, do I want to have a relationship with him? Sometimes I do, when I am confident and trusting, or when I'm not thinking about some girl I shouldn't be thinking about, but other times I don't really want a relationship with God at all. Being in a relationship with God can feel invasive, bigger than choosing a roommate or a spouse, more encompassing, in fact. To have a relationship with God, you have to give up freedom and control, I think. And while the benefits of the relationship may be great, all relationship comes with some cost.

But Jesus wants a relationship all the same. In fact, it's nearly all he wants. He wants us to know him, to interact with him, and even to be one with him. And he doesn't want this because he is

lonely. He wants this because he knows how much *we* need this relationship. We see elements of this in a conversation Jesus has with a woman at a well:

Therefore, when the Lord knew that the Pharisees had heard that Jesus made and baptized more disciples than John (though Jesus Himself did not baptize, but His disciples), He left Judea and departed again to Galilee. But He needed to go through Samaria.

So He came to a city of Samaria which is called Sychar, near the plot of ground that Jacob gave to his son Joseph. Now Jacob's well was there. Jesus therefore, being wearied from His journey, sat thus by the well. It was about the sixth hour.

A woman of Samaria came to draw water. Jesus said to her, "Give Me a drink." For His disciples had gone away into the city to buy food.

Then the woman of Samaria said to Him, "How is it that You, being a Jew, ask a drink from me, a Samaritan woman?" For Jews have no dealings with Samaritans.

Jesus answered and said to her, "If you knew the gift of God, and who it is who says to you, 'Give Me a drink,' you would have asked Him, and He would have given you living water."

The woman said to Him, "Sir, You have nothing to draw with, and the well is deep. Where then do You get that living water? Are You greater than our father Jacob, who gave us the well, and drank from it himself, as well as his sons and his livestock?"

Jesus answered and said to her, "Whoever drinks of this water will thirst again, but whoever drinks of the water that I shall give him will never thirst. But the water that I shall give him will become in him a fountain of water springing up into everlasting life."

The woman said to Him, "Sir, give me this water, that I may not thirst, nor come here to draw."

Jesus said to her, "Go, call your husband, and come here."

The woman answered and said, "I have no husband."

Jesus said to her, "You have well said, 'I have no husband,' for you have had five husbands, and the one whom you now have is not your husband; in that you spoke truly."

The woman said to Him, "Sir, I perceive that You are a prophet. Our fathers worshiped on this mountain, and you Jews say that in Jerusalem is the place where one ought to worship."

Jesus said to her, "Woman, believe Me, the hour is coming when you will neither on this mountain, nor in Jerusalem, worship the Father. You worship what you do not know; we know what we worship, for salvation is of the Jews. But the hour is coming, and now is, when the true worshipers will worship the Father in spirit and truth; for the Father is seeking such to worship Him. God is Spirit, and those who worship Him must worship in spirit and truth."

The woman said to Him, "I know that Messiah is coming" (who is called Christ). "When He comes, He will tell us all things."

Jesus said to her, "I who speak to you am He." (John 4:1–26)

As the apostle John begins this story, he tells us why Jesus leaves Judea to return to Galilee. He inserts an editorial comment that gives perspective to the whole story and helps us discover the lessons John wants to teach. He says, "But He (Jesus) needed to go through Samaria."

Now the interesting thing is, Jesus didn't *have* to go through Samaria to return to Galilee. There was no geographical reason for Jesus to go through Samaria. In fact, Jews traveling this route rarely, if ever, went through Samaria. They had a strong prejudice against Samarians and went to great lengths to avoid traveling through their neighborhoods.

And so this meeting between Jesus and the woman at the well happened because Jesus went out of his way to interact with this marginalized community, and perhaps with this specific woman. Regardless, he sought her out in order to establish a relationship with her. In fact, their entire conversation focuses on relationship. He talks about the men she's lived with, and tells

her, in a sense, that he knows those relationships haven't been satisfying.

Jesus offers himself as living water for her, and by this he indicates his would be a different kind of relationship, one that wouldn't get old and unsatisfying. It would be very different, not romantic like the others, not earthly, but something more, something greater.

What would be the key to this relationship? Worship. Jesus talks about worship, and so explains, in part, that our relationship with him will be a worshipful relationship. We worship when we agree with who he says he is, understand he is God, agree that he is good, and give him the praise he is due.

What I love about this passage is that God isn't standing far off in a distant palace demanding that people worship him. He makes these statements after having gone out of his way to pursue a woman who could cost him his reputation. Jesus invites her to worship him and enter into a relationship that would be different and satisfying.

"But the hour is coming, and now is, when the true worshipers will worship the Father in spirit and truth; for the Father is seeking such to worship Him" (John 4:23). God *seeks* true worshipers. God *pursues* us. That's why Jesus had to go through Samaria. This unusual route was another example of Jesus *pursuing* relationships with people. I imagine Jesus smiling to his disciples, knowing why he was going this particular way, and saying, "Come on, you guys, we need to go this way." Then thinking silently to himself, *There's someone I want to meet.*

Closing Thoughts

How has Jesus ever gone out of his way to pursue you?

Small Group Discussion Questions

These questions will be discussed at your small group meeting.

1. *If the Jesus captured in John 2:1–11 was who he claimed to be, the Son of God and God himself in the flesh, does John's story help you believe he might accept you as you are? (See Day 1.)*

2. *In all honesty, is it hard to believe God both knows you and cares about you?*

If so, why is it hard to believe God can be caring? Why is it hard to believe he can care about you? (See Day 2.)

3. *What would a world without justice look like?*

What would happen if our government did not have a system of checks and balances? (See Day 3.)

4. *Do you find the idea of a fair and merciful judge comforting?*

How does this passage change the idea of God's judgment for you? (See Day 3.)

5. How much of our distrust of people probably comes from insecurity?

Are some of our feelings that God doesn't like us also born from insecurities?

What would life look like if we actually believed that the God who made us liked us, enjoyed being around us, and wanted to be our friend? (See Day 4.)

6. *Does part of you entertain the idea that God has pursued you?*

What evidence do you see that God wants a relationship with you?

How does it make you feel to know the God of the universe may be pursuing you?

What would it look like to worship him? (See Day 5.)

Did you have any other questions from the reading you'd like to discuss with the group? If so, write them here:

Do You Think Life Is What It Ought to Be?

Opening Thoughts

- What was your first experience with darkness or tragedy?

- Where do you think God is in our darkest moments?

- When have you seen Christ enter into your suffering?

■ Day 1: Houston, Do We Have a Problem?

I think it was Sartre who said the problem with the world is other people. I couldn't agree more. I'm kidding, of course, and so was Sartre I am sure, but it's true there is something deep within the human spirit that contends with itself and with the spirit of others. It's not very definable, but there is an insatiable desire within every human being to be affirmed and validated; and when we are not, things go haywire. It isn't always violent, but it's almost always sad. The Bible calls this problem "sin." But when the Bible talks about sin, it's hardly the kind of sin you might think of when you hear the word. Christians use the word *sin*, often, to judge other people and to feel superior. That behavior, interestingly enough, is also sin. Even Christians can't get away from it. But what is sin? Is it lust, greed, jealousy, and prejudice, or are those things just symptoms of a greater, deeper problem? The Bible would suggest the actions we commonly think of as sin are actually manifestations of a broken inner condition. And our broken inner condition couldn't be more obvious. In fact,

G. K. Chesterton said, "The only bit of Christian theology you can actually prove is the existence of sin!"

I've heard people say man is born good, and society makes him bad. And to some degree I think this is true, because unhealthy societies, communities, and families definitely affect us. But the Bible might say unhealthy societies, communities, and families just make the problem worse. And the problem is able to be made worse because we were broken to begin with, or, more pointedly, we were already bent toward self-absorption. This doesn't mean we are bad in the classic usage of the word, because we still love our children and our spouses and are very charitable people. I think it just means that when somebody pulls out in front of us on the road, God wouldn't put it past us to flip the guy off.

One of the reasons it's hard to believe we have a sin nature is because we live in a civilized society. America has its problems, but the truth is, we aren't that bad. I often forget the genius of the American system has little to do with freedom. Congress is watching the Senate, the Senate is watching Congress, and both are watching the Executive Branch, which is all being watched by the nightly news, which in turn is being watched by you, who vote to elect the leaders who appoint judges to rule on cases the police bring before them at the hearing of which you stand and explain the light was in fact yellow. The genius of the American system isn't freedom, then; it's checks and balances. The truth is, if we weren't all watching each other, it would be *Lord of the Flies.*

The truth is, our forefathers were on to something. What they realized is that a human being, if left unchecked, will often make decisions in the interest of self. I don't think this is a black-and-white rule, because if we were alone on a street at night and saw a crying baby all alone on the side of the road, we'd instinctively run over and see what was wrong. But the idea there is something inherently selfish about the human heart is not difficult to dispute. If it weren't so, we wouldn't have police departments; we'd just all agree to not speed.

We'd do this over a handshake and a beer and that would settle it.

Thoughtful people throughout human history have pondered the problem of human nature. Most of the conversation, regardless of religious or cultural differences, has produced amazing agreement. The consensus is this: what we are on the "inside" is the truest measure of ourselves. An ancient proverb says it this way: "As water reflects a face, so a man's heart reflects the man" (Proverbs 27:19 NIV).

I don't have kids, but I joked with a friend who had recently had a second child that he should do an experiment. I told him to properly reward and discipline one child and then leave the other one alone. By that I meant he and his wife should not instruct the child on what is commonly considered right or wrong behavior. I said this to my friend because he mentioned he believed we are all essentially good and it is culture that makes us bad. I figured if we are all essentially good, then he shouldn't have to train his kid at all. And when his two-year-old screams "mine," he can just blame it on that terrible street gang his two-year-old has fallen in with. You know, the ones at the play center at McDonald's.

I only say all this because Scripture has something to say about our natures, and most people don't like to hear it. Jesus' view of humanity is consistent throughout the stories and events in which we meet him. He assumes we are in trouble. He sees us as self-destructive. No one is exempt. Listen to his verdict: "Light has come into the world, and men loved darkness rather than light, because their deeds were evil" (John 3:19).

Notice Jesus doesn't say men do dark or bad things. He says we *love* the darkness. Ultimately the root problem with the world is found inside each of us. We live and act the way we do because it is our nature, our sinful nature. Sin is a heart problem long before it becomes a behavior problem. So change in the

world must be internal, not external. Many religious communities who study the Bible fail to understand this issue. But the truth is, if we change our thoughts, feelings, and motivations, our behaviors and actions will change as well.

Jesus presents this idea with the tenderness and directness of a doctor who is diagnosing a fatal illness. He states it as a fact and prescribes a treatment plan. We see him saying to the woman at the well, "Go and sin no more," and to the woman caught in adultery he says the same thing. He tells the Pharisees they are like whitewashed tombs, clean on the outside yet dead on the inside. They (and we) need a new nature. Modifying or changing our behavior alone will not do. We need to change what we are *essentially*.

Were it not for checks and balances in your life, who do you think you would be? Would you be spoiled? Would you be unruly? If selfish behavior didn't cost you something, do you think you'd still be unselfish? Jesus would contend that compassion, kindness, and altruism must be taught, that these things are counter to our nature. He would also contend that even though these things can be taught, we are still very broken, and something surgical needs to be done to our hearts to make things right. And we will get to that soon.

Closing Thoughts

Can you catch yourself thinking selfish thoughts? Do you think Jesus' idea that there is something fundamentally broken about us is true?

■ Day 2: Do We Really Need God to Help Us?

In Scripture Jesus talks a great deal about hunger and thirst. He said to the Samaritan woman at the well, "Whoever drinks of the water that I shall give him will never thirst" (John 4:14). And in John 6:35 Jesus says, "I am the bread of life. He who comes to Me shall never hunger." In these passages, Jesus is talking about more than physical food and water. He is talking about something spiritual, something for which we all long. We have dreams and goals. We desire love, acceptance, and accomplishment. We want to be in relationship, make a difference, or have our voice heard. It is what we fill up our hours with—the *striving* and *doing* of life.

Jesus pointed to this deeper need when he spoke to crowds of people near the Sea of Galilee. Here's what happened:

When the people therefore saw that Jesus was not there, nor His disciples, they also got into boats and came to Capernaum, seeking Jesus. And when they found Him on the other side of the sea, they said to Him, "Rabbi, when did You come here?"

Jesus answered them and said, "Most assuredly, I say to you, you seek Me, not because you saw the signs, but because you ate of the loaves and were filled. Do not labor for the food which perishes, but for the food which endures to everlasting life, which the Son of Man will give you, because God the Father has set His seal on Him."

Then they said to Him, "What shall we do, that we may work the works of God?"

Jesus answered and said to them, "This is the work of God, that you believe in Him whom He sent."

Therefore they said to Him, "What sign will You perform then, that we may see it and believe You? What work will You do? Our fathers ate the manna in the desert; as it is written, 'He gave them bread from heaven to eat.'"

Then Jesus said to them, "Most assuredly, I say to you, Moses did not give you the bread from heaven, but My Father

gives you the true bread from heaven. For the bread of God is
He who comes down from heaven and gives life to the world."
Then they said to Him, "Lord, give us this bread always."
And Jesus said to them, "I am the bread of life. He who
comes to Me shall never hunger, and he who believes in Me
shall never thirst." (John 6:24–35)

This deeper longing of our souls isn't a need for friendship,
really, or even for romance, though those needs exist. The need
Jesus talks about is a need for God. Just as we need water
and food for physical life, we need love, purpose, significance,
acceptance, hope, and belonging for our heart life, and Jesus
tells us that these things can only come from God. But he's
compassionate toward us. He understands that, just like the
Samaritan woman, we struggle to meet our needs by filling our
lives with people and places instead of turning to him for our
satisfaction.

Jesus refers to this confusing search of ours as a kind of
blindness. He said on more than one occasion, "I am the light of
the world" (John 8:12; 9:5). In a world that is dark and confusing,
we are unable to see things as they really are. But when Jesus
invades our lives, his Spirit working in us is the light that will allow
us to see.

When we deny Christ access to our lives, we remain in
bondage to the darkness and to our own nature. And we *eat*
and *drink* the stuff that will never fulfill us. This explains why we
can't stop doing the bad we don't want to do. We are longing
for something, and the longing is insatiable. Like Edmund's
"turkish delight" in C. S. Lewis's classic children's story *The Lion,
the Witch, and the Wardrobe*, the food we are feeding on
leaves us always hungry. And we are so blind we can't even see
what's happening.

Are we left to wander and stumble in the darkness we love,
blind to our perilous condition?

Jesus says it doesn't have to be this way. In John 8:32, Jesus says, "You shall know the truth, and the truth shall make you free." When we know Jesus, really know him, we find a new freedom to discover fulfillment and satisfaction by acting and living in his will. This brings us back to yesterday's conversation—change must start on the interior for change to occur on the exterior.

Remember what Jesus said:

"Whoever drinks of the water I shall give him will never thirst" (John 4:14).

"I am the bread of life. He who comes to Me shall never hunger" (John 6:35).

"I am the light of the world" (John 8:12).

Jesus will satisfy your spiritual thirst, your spiritual hunger, and he will be light in your darkness. Interestingly, his answer to the world's problems is not religious. It's not a philosophy or a list of rules. The answer to our problem is in *him*. Jesus claims he is the truth, and he will set us free.

Many times, our longing is hidden even from ourselves. Our hope is placed in career or other relationships, but often that's all it is—hope. And hope, as we all know, is often false hope. But Jesus offers something different, *a hope that will not disappoint.*

Closing Thoughts

Do you feel longing for something greater in life, something that life just doesn't seem to have in it?

■ Day 3: What Do You Hope For?

If you think about it, we are all living on hope. If you were to make a list of the things you hope for right now, you'd probably be surprised at how extensive it would be. We hope for something better in our relationships, for our kids, in our jobs, in our living situations. We hope the movie we are going to see is funny or that dinner at a new restaurant will be good, and so on and so on. Very few people are satisfied, and most of us think we will only be satisfied *if* and *when*.

Hoping for something to make things a little better stems from the inner brokenness Jesus talks about. We know something is not quite right in our lives. It's hard to put a finger on, but we have a constant suspicion that life needs a little tweaking.

One of the greatest stories of hope I've ever read is the account of Jesus' death. Yes, you read me right. And I know that sounds odd, finding hope in death, but if you'll read Luke 23:32–43, you'll see what I mean. The account goes something like this . . .

Jesus was tortured and viciously executed on a tree. There were two other men, criminals, who hung on either side of him. As Jesus was dying and in unimaginable pain, he asked God to forgive his executioners. This, to me, seems like a remarkably hopeful thing for the Son of God to do. He forgave those who were in the process of torturing and killing him. Even though this is all very dark, I say it brings me hope because it means that God is more forgiving than I could possibly imagine.

His gracious nature continues in the account of his death. The crowd that had gathered yelled at him and mocked him. They sneered and hurled insults at him as the weight of his body hung from the nails and tore at his hands and feet. And the criminal who was hanging on one side of him joined them, using his dying breath to mock this man who claimed to be God.

But the criminal on the other side of Jesus had a very honest moment. Perhaps, there in the last few minutes of his own life, he believed Jesus was who he said he was, and perhaps after hearing Jesus forgive those who had tortured and crucified him, he knew God was a God of mercy. He recognized his own guilt and rebuked the other man, saying, "We are getting what we deserve."

His death now imminent and unavoidable, this criminal threw himself on the only possible hope he had left. He simply said, "Jesus, remember me."

Jesus' answer is as incredible as anything I've ever heard. Not only did he promise to remember this man, he did infinitely more than that. He promised the criminal that they would be together on the other side of this life.

Why would Luke want to include this story in his narrative? What does it contribute to his portrayal of Jesus? I believe it is this: here is proof that when all hope is truly gone, when you come to the end of your life and see nothing has worked except to temporarily satisfy, Jesus not only is one whom you can find hope in but—miracle of miracles—*will* fulfill your hope beyond your greatest dreams. The apostle Paul says it best when he says the hope that we have in Christ will not disappoint (see Romans 5:5).

Don't get me wrong: hope doesn't make us instantly happy. That is not what Jesus is saying. The hope we have in Christ is in knowing that he will bring closure to the mess we are living in. But what a beautiful hope that is. It means when everybody else is panicking, trying to stuff their lives with things that will eventually leave them unsatisfied, we can rest assured that the closure we need—the forgiveness, the love and affirmation, the end to our internal struggle—will be delivered by Christ.

Jesus offers hope to the hopeless. And to those who dare to hope in him, he *delivers.*

Closing Thoughts

What are some things you hope in that simply haven't worked? Have you placed too much hope in those things? What do you think about Jesus' invitation to place your hope in him?

■ Day 4: Lost

Have you ever been driving and realized you didn't know where you were and you didn't know how to get where you wanted to go? Even when I know that I'm lost, I have a hard time admitting it . . . especially to whichever friend may be riding with me at the time.

I think this may be related to the reason some people didn't like Jesus. They had trouble admitting they were lost. Jesus didn't soft-sell the idea that people are lost either. He said it clearly: you are blind; you cannot see. And some people simply walked away. But others didn't. Those who recognized they were blind and were willing to admit it to themselves and others were able to trust Jesus to help them.

Jesus knows we're lost. He repeatedly said he came to rescue us. The words the Gospel writers use most often are *redeem* and *save*. For example, see Luke 19:10: "The Son of Man has come to seek and to save that which was lost."

Being lost shouldn't surprise or offend us. I have a hard time finding my keys every other time I leave the house. Do I think I'm really going to find the meaning of life on my own, without help? Or bigger yet, could I possibly encounter God if he doesn't come to me first? It would be easier to figure out quantum physics.

Consider Luke 15:3–6:

So He spoke this parable to them, saying:

"What man of you, having a hundred sheep, if he loses one of them, does not leave the ninety-nine in the wilderness, and go after the one which is lost until he finds it? And when he has found it, he lays it on his shoulders, rejoicing. And when he comes home, he calls together his friends and neighbors, saying to them, 'Rejoice with me, for I have found my sheep which was lost!'"

In the parable of the lost sheep, we see again the gracious and merciful nature of Jesus. Does God scold the sheep and make him feel guilty for getting lost? Does God send the sheep to map-reading school to learn how not to get lost? Does God let the sheep stay lost? No. A thousand times, no. He has mercy.

If you've ever worked with sheep (or heard from people who work with sheep), you know that without a shepherd, the sheep will surely die. They simply aren't smart enough to find the good grass, stay out of crags, or keep themselves safe from wolves.

As a student of Scripture, Jesus certainly would have had this verse in the back of his head as he told this story: "We are His people and the sheep of His pasture" (Psalm 100:3). This story is for all of us human beings, including you and me. All of us have wandered from the fold of God's love at some point. And yet, like a shepherd who will go to any length to find his lost sheep, God will seek you out. And when he finds you he will rescue you from whatever you've gotten yourself into. He will rescue you and take you home. Jesus is the shepherd we need.

Religion would tell you you've screwed up and now you have to find a way out. This appeals to most of us. We like the idea of fixing the mess we've gotten ourselves into. We don't like

the idea of needing anybody to rescue us. But the lostness that Jesus has come to rescue us from is far more terrible than getting lost while driving or wandering away from a literal sheep herd. The lostness Jesus talks about is a lostness of the soul. This kind of lostness ruins our lives and the lives of our families and everybody around us. Not to mention, they are lost too.

How comforting is it, then, that there is a God who will come after us? Jesus didn't come to give us directions so we could find the way ourselves. He didn't come to teach us the right way to go. He didn't invent ten rules to follow so you wouldn't get lost. He doesn't show us a way to our destination. He comes and gets us.

Again, like his provision for our spiritual hunger, God offers to satisfy this need with himself. Jesus says, "You are lost, but I am the way to the Father. Not a system, not a religion, but a person. All you have to do is know me, and you are no longer lost."

Closing Thoughts

Do you sometimes feel lost?

■ Day 5: Life Without a Net?

The last and greatest question we all face is the question of death.

Is this life all there is?

We've all seen famous people interviewed on TV after the death of a fellow celebrity. People who generally have no place for faith in their lives or no consideration of life after death in their daily lives will say things like, "I know he is in a better place." The truth is, we all long for something more than our eighty short years on the planet.

What's really, really great about Jesus is that he doesn't ignore or avoid this question. He meets it head-on with the greatest news anyone has ever given.

Now a certain man was sick, Lazarus of Bethany, the town of Mary and her sister Martha. It was that Mary who anointed the Lord with fragrant oil and wiped His feet with her hair, whose brother Lazarus was sick. Therefore the sisters sent to Him, saying, "Lord, behold, he whom You love is sick."

When Jesus heard that, He said, "This sickness is not unto death, but for the glory of God, that the Son of God may be glorified through it."

Now Jesus loved Martha and her sister and Lazarus. So, when He heard that he was sick, He stayed two more days in the place where He was. Then after this He said to the disciples, "Let us go to Judea again."

The disciples said to Him, "Rabbi, lately the Jews sought to stone You, and are You going there again?"

Jesus answered, "Are there not twelve hours in the day? If anyone walks in the day, he does not stumble, because he sees the light of this world. But if one walks in the night, he stumbles, because the light is not in him." These things He said, and after that He said to them, "Our friend Lazarus sleeps, but I go that I may wake him up."

Then His disciples said, "Lord, if he sleeps he will get well." However, Jesus spoke of his death, but they thought that He was speaking about taking rest in sleep.

Then Jesus said to them plainly, "Lazarus is dead. And I am glad for your sakes that I was not there, that you may believe. Nevertheless let us go to him."

Then Thomas, who is called the Twin, said to his fellow disciples, "Let us also go, that we may die with Him."

So when Jesus came, He found that he had already been in the tomb four days. Now Bethany was near Jerusalem, about two miles away. And many of the Jews had joined the women around Martha and Mary, to comfort them concerning their brother.

Now Martha, as soon as she heard that Jesus was coming, went and met Him, but Mary was sitting in the house. Now Martha said to Jesus, "Lord, if You had been here, my brother would not have died. But even now I know that whatever You ask of God, God will give You."

Jesus said to her, "Your brother will rise again."

Martha said to Him, "I know that he will rise again in the resurrection at the last day."

Jesus said to her, "I am the resurrection and the life. He who believes in Me, though he may die, he shall live. And whoever lives and believes in Me shall never die. Do you believe this?"

She said to Him, "Yes, Lord, I believe that You are the Christ, the Son of God, who is to come into the world."

And when she had said these things, she went her way and secretly called Mary her sister, saying, "The Teacher has come and is calling for you." As soon as she heard that, she arose quickly and came to Him. Now Jesus had not yet come into the town, but was in the place where Martha met Him. Then the Jews who were with her in the house, and comforting her, when they saw that Mary rose up quickly and went out, followed her, saying, "She is going to the tomb to weep there."

Then, when Mary came where Jesus was, and saw Him, she fell down at His feet, saying to Him, "Lord, if You had been here, my brother would not have died."

Therefore, when Jesus saw her weeping, and the Jews who came with her weeping, He groaned in the spirit and was troubled. And He said, "Where have you laid him?"

They said to Him, "Lord, come and see."

Jesus wept. Then the Jews said, "See how He loved him!"

And some of them said, "Could not this Man, who opened the eyes of the blind, also have kept this man from dying?"

Then Jesus, again groaning in Himself, came to the tomb. It was a cave, and a stone lay against it. Jesus said, "Take away the stone."

Martha, the sister of him who was dead, said to Him, "Lord, by this time there is a stench, for he has been dead four days."

Jesus said to her, "Did I not say to you that if you would believe you would see the glory of God?" Then they took away the stone from the place where the dead man was lying. And Jesus lifted up His eyes and said, "Father, I thank You that You have heard Me. And I know that You always hear Me, but because of the people who are standing by I said this, that they may believe that You sent Me." Now when He had said these things, He cried with a loud voice, "Lazarus, come forth!" And he who had died came out bound hand and foot with graveclothes, and his face was wrapped with a cloth. Jesus said to them, "Loose him, and let him go." (John 11:1–44)

Jesus waited for Lazarus to die. Odd. A bit scary. But he does this so you and I *will see what God is like.* This is crucial. We need to be convinced. This is *the* big one. You can't mess with death. We don't get a do-over.

Martha comes running to Jesus, and even when you're reading the story you can almost hear how out of breath she is: "Lord, if You had been here, my brother would not have died."

Imagine the compassion with which Jesus looks at Martha. (John has told us twice that Jesus loved this family (vv. 3, 5).) He says, "Your brother will rise again."

John tells us Martha deflects this statement and tries to come up with a good religious answer. Jesus patiently hears her and

then drops the bomb, "(Martha,) I am the resurrection and the life. He who believes in Me, though he may die, he shall live." Then full of grace and love, Jesus looks her straight in the eye and asks her the question of all questions: "Do you believe this?"

Martha, who in grief is a bit confused between hope and religion, comes up with a brilliant answer. In fact, it's the point of the entire narrative for John (see 20:30–31). She says, "Yes, Lord, I believe You are the Christ, the Son of God, who is to come into the world."

Jesus then raises Lazarus from the dead. But the miracle is not necessarily the point of the story. The point is, God wants you and me to know the last and greatest enemy of man is not to be feared. Jesus has an answer—he is someone who is greater than death. And he loves you. And he looks into our eyes, as he did Martha, and asks, "Do you believe me?"

Closing Thoughts

Do you believe Jesus lives outside death and has power over death?

Small Group Discussion Questions

These questions will be discussed at your small group meeting.

1. *Do you think human nature tends to lean toward self-interest?*

If all the checks and balances were removed from your life, would you be able to regulate your nature and basically be a good person? (See Day 1.)

2. How do you see Jesus' proposition, that we are essentially broken people, played out in your life and in your relationships? (See Day 1.)

3. Have you experienced the spiritual hunger and thirst that Jesus talks about?

The woman at the well believed Jesus was who he said he was. She went and told the people in the town that she had met the Son of God. At this point in our study, who do you think Jesus is?

Are you interested in Jesus being water and food to your spiritual hunger and thirst? (See Day 2.)

4. In the past, in what people or things have you placed your hope?

When the criminal dying next to Christ asked Jesus to remember him, did you find yourself also hoping Jesus would remember you?

Do you believe that if you ask Jesus to remember you, and trust his mercy to forgive you of all your sins, he will do it? (See Day 3.)

5. *Do you believe that if you were lost, Jesus would come and find you?*

Do you believe that through this study, through all these things Jesus is saying to you, he has come to find you?

How do you respond to Jesus as he reaches out and says, "I am the way, and the truth, and the life. No one comes to the Father except through Me" (John 14:6)?

6. *How do you respond to Jesus' sadness at Lazarus's death?*

Why do you think Jesus waited so long to arrive at their house?

How does his miracle two thousand years ago comfort you today? (See Day 5.)

Will God Break into Our Lives?

Opening Thoughts

- Do you fear being known personally and intimately?
- Do you think God has a right to be involved in your life?
- In what ways do you shut God out of your life?

■ Day 1: God Breaks into the Lives of the Worst of Us

Then Jesus entered and passed through Jericho. Now behold, there was a man named Zacchaeus who was a chief tax collector, and he was rich. And he sought to see who Jesus was, but could not because of the crowd, for he was of short stature. So he ran ahead and climbed up into a sycamore tree to see Him, for He was going to pass that way. And when Jesus came to the place, He looked up and saw him, and said to him, "Zacchaeus, make haste and come down, for today I must stay at your house." So he made haste and came down, and received Him joyfully. But when they saw it, they all complained, saying, "He has gone to be a guest with a man who is a sinner."

Then Zacchaeus stood and said to the Lord, "Look, Lord, I give half of my goods to the poor; and if I have taken anything from anyone by false accusation, I restore fourfold."

And Jesus said to him, "Today salvation has come to this house, because he also is a son of Abraham; for the Son of

Man has come to seek and to save that which was lost." (Luke 19:1–10)

Of the many things I enjoy about the Bible, one is the fact that it doesn't play politics. The Bible does not read like a careful brochure, only telling us the fashionable things about Jesus. Take this great scene in Luke, for example. Jesus befriended Zacchaeus, a person who nearly everybody despised because of his job as chief tax collector. He was quite wealthy, and we can assume his wealth came from large amounts of money he added to people's tax bills and then kept for himself. You can imagine his reputation—just think of corrupt government officials today. But Jesus didn't care; he befriended Zacchaeus all the same.

In the account, Jesus was walking through Jericho and the crowd surrounding him was so large Zacchaeus couldn't get a view. So he ran ahead and climbed a tree to get a glimpse of the rabbi. Luke tells us when Jesus saw Zacchaeus, he stopped and demanded Zacchaeus have him over to his house for dinner. Jesus did this in public, for everybody to see and hear. The crowd must have been shocked. Imagine, a prominent religious figure wanting to have dinner at the home of someone who was stealing money from the poor. It was obvious Jesus wasn't going to be running for office anytime soon. The rumors must have flown through Jericho instantly. And not only this, but by choosing Zacchaeus to host him for dinner, Jesus, as a popular rabbi, bestowed honor on him.

This explains Zacchaeus's reaction of "receiv(ing) Him joyfully."

You can almost hear the contempt in the voices of the crowd when you read, "He has gone to be a guest with a man who is a sinner." What this amounts to is this: Jesus picked the least liked person in town, someone who was universally despised and hated. And Jesus befriended him. Amazing!

But why? We can only suppose Jesus saw the heart inside Zacchaeus, saw he was desperately lost. Jesus wanted to befriend that heart.

Luke's point comes at the end of verse 10: "For the Son of Man has come to seek and to save that which was lost." Jesus doesn't seek out the best of us. He breaks into the lives of the *worst* of us. In this scene with Zacchaeus, Jesus once again proves that this is the kind of God he is.

Are there things in your life that cause you to believe Jesus would not or could never break into it? No matter how bad or broken we believe ourselves to be, Jesus seeks us out so he might redeem us. Even the worst of us.

Closing Thoughts

Do you think Jesus couldn't or wouldn't rescue you? Why?

■ Day 2: God Heals Even When We Have Lost Our
Hope for Healing

There have probably been times in all our lives when we've felt hopeless. When we were young, it may have been something simple, like rejection from a girlfriend or boyfriend. But as we grew older, and for some of us not too much older, life may have taken a turn. It might have been the loss of a friend or a car accident that took part of who you were before. Or

you may have come to the slow realization that the people who were supposed to protect you didn't. For whatever reason and in whatever way, outside forces came and made our lives more difficult as we grew older. For some of us, this has caused us to lose hope.

Under the weight of the pressure that life brings, many people experience seasons of hopelessness. We may not live there all the time, but divorce, bankruptcy, or the loss of our health can put us in a dark place where there seems to be no light, and no way out.

> After this there was a feast of the Jews, and Jesus went up to Jerusalem. Now there is in Jerusalem by the Sheep Gate a pool, which is called in Hebrew, Bethesda, having five porches. In these lay a great multitude of sick people, blind, lame, paralyzed, waiting for the moving of the water. For an angel went down at a certain time into the pool and stirred up the water; then whoever stepped in first, after the stirring of the water, was made well of whatever disease he had. Now a certain man was there who had an infirmity thirty-eight years. When Jesus saw him lying there, and knew that he already had been in that condition a long time, He said to him, "Do you want to be made well?"
>
> The sick man answered Him, "Sir, I have no man to put me into the pool when the water is stirred up; but while I am coming, another steps down before me."
>
> Jesus said to him, "Rise, take up your bed and walk." And immediately the man was made well, took up his bed, and walked. And that day was the Sabbath. (John 5:1–9)

The man we meet in John 5 had a very real problem. He had been paralyzed for thirty-eight years. He was a man who, by all accounts, should not have had any hope. He was lying by a pool where he believed he could find healing. It was supposed to be a magical pool where people went and dipped in the water in order to be healed. We don't know whether people were actually healed at this pool or if it was just superstition (John doesn't bother telling us), but just the fact that he was there tells us he wanted something more. What was amazing is that after thirty-eight years he was still trying.

Jesus sought out this man and asked him a question, of which we, the readers, already know the answer: "Do you want to get well?"

What a strange question to ask. Of course he wanted to get well. Perhaps Jesus was really saying, "Do you still have hope?" John had a point in relating this story. We know the man was lying by the pool so he could be healed, and the man answered, "I have no one to help me in the pool." You can almost hear the fragility in the man's voice when he says this. There is no one to care for him; he is alone.

Interestingly, the man didn't answer Jesus' question with a "Why do you ask?" or "Can you help me?" Here was an opportunity for this hopeless and lonely man to trust Jesus instead of the magic waters of the pool. But he didn't know who Jesus was. He just thought this guy might help him get into the pool.

No matter. Jesus told him, "Get up! Pick up your mat and walk." Notice, carefully, the paralytic was healed *completely* and *immediately*. He acted in faith and did exactly what Jesus had told him to do.

But the emphasis here is not on the man's faith. It is on how Jesus revealed God's character. This man had endured the suffering of being paralyzed for thirty-eight years. He was alone in a world that saw him as an outcast. He had no one to help him. But God knew his misery. He knew his hopelessness. And he broke into his life without so much as an invitation to do so.

Now we want to be very clear here. The point of this story is not that God heals people whenever they want. In fact, this man had been paralyzed for decades. Instead, John's point is to demonstrate the character of God through Jesus—that God heals, that he desires to make things whole. Add this to the other

idea Jesus teaches in that the real problems we face are not external, but internal, and the passage means all the more.

Closing Thoughts

Do you believe God wants to heal something in your life?

■ Day 3: God Has No Prejudice

In Week 1 we glimpsed into the life of the Samaritan woman, whose life Jesus changed radically in an encounter at the town well. Now we're returning to her story to examine a new aspect of God's character. Here's the passage again as a refresher:

> Therefore, when the Lord knew that the Pharisees had heard that Jesus made and baptized more disciples than John (though Jesus Himself did not baptize, but His disciples), He left Judea and departed again to Galilee. But He needed to go through Samaria.
>
> So He came to a city of Samaria which is called Sychar, near the plot of ground that Jacob gave to his son Joseph. Now Jacob's well was there. Jesus therefore, being wearied from His journey, sat thus by the well. It was about the sixth hour.
>
> A woman of Samaria came to draw water. Jesus said to her, "Give Me a drink." For His disciples had gone away into the city to buy food.

Then the woman of Samaria said to Him, "How is it that You, being a Jew, ask a drink from me, a Samaritan woman?" For Jews have no dealings with Samaritans.

Jesus answered and said to her, "If you knew the gift of God, and who it is who says to you, 'Give Me a drink,' you would have asked Him, and He would have given you living water."

The woman said to Him, "Sir, You have nothing to draw with, and the well is deep. Where then do You get that living water? Are You greater than our father Jacob, who gave us the well, and drank from it himself, as well as his sons and his livestock?"

Jesus answered and said to her, "Whoever drinks of this water will thirst again, but whoever drinks of the water that I shall give him will never thirst. But the water that I shall give him will become in him a fountain of water springing up into everlasting life."

The woman said to Him, "Sir, give me this water, that I may not thirst, nor come here to draw."

Jesus said to her, "Go, call your husband, and come here."

The woman answered and said, "I have no husband."

Jesus said to her, "You have well said, 'I have no husband,' for you have had five husbands, and the one whom you now have is not your husband; in that you spoke truly."

The woman said to Him, "Sir, I perceive that You are a prophet. Our fathers worshiped on this mountain, and you Jews say that in Jerusalem is the place where one ought to worship."

Jesus said to her, "Woman, believe Me, the hour is coming when you will neither on this mountain, nor in Jerusalem, worship the Father. You worship what you do not know; we know what we worship, for salvation is of the Jews. But the hour is coming, and now is, when the true worshipers will worship the Father in spirit and truth; for the Father is seeking such to worship Him. God is Spirit, and those who worship Him must worship in spirit and truth."

The woman said to Him, "I know that Messiah is coming" (who is called Christ). "When He comes, He will tell us all things."

Jesus said to her, "I who speak to you am He." (John 4:1–26)

Christian theology asserts that because of the fall of man, we constantly compare ourselves to others. Without a relationship with God, we are trying to figure out why we matter. And because we compare ourselves to others, we often devalue people for seemingly insignificant reasons. This explains racism and socioeconomic prejudice, and why your aunt Hazel won't talk to your aunt Margaret because your cousin Ethel married that kid who ran for city council under the Green Party.

In the story about the Samaritan woman, John tells us Jews do not associate with Samaritans. What he is saying is they had a prejudice. Jews considered Samaritans to be heretics, members of a cult, and untouchable. But Jesus doesn't subscribe to such barriers. He sees them as illusions in the minds of broken people. He sees them as lies.

It seems to me that since I was a very small child I have always compared myself to others. Even when I was in elementary school it seemed like, in my mind, we were always lining up from best to worse. Whether in sports, looks, intellect, or personality, there was an ongoing contest of comparison.

I was on a bus once and there was a man sitting near me who smelled. He hadn't bathed in days, and as I looked away from him it occurred to me Jesus would have the humility to interact with him. And then I realized this thought was terribly arrogant. I should not have the *humility* to interact with him, as though the man were less than I. I simply should have seen him as an equal. Jesus wouldn't have interacted with this man out of humility; he would have done so out of enjoyment, because he wouldn't see him as any less than anybody else.

We see this in Jesus' interaction with the Samaritan woman. He asks her for a drink. This is not a demeaning, chauvinist request. It's much more scandalous than that. Jews, especially rabbis, were to have nothing to do with Samaritans. And yet Jesus intentionally goes to the well to interact with this woman. He doesn't merely make polite small talk; he engages in a very vulnerable conversation with her. Jesus knows intimate details of her life—specifically the men she had slept with. The woman must have been surprised, wondering how he had so quickly engaged local rumors. And yet Jesus does not demean her. Instead, he makes a very strange offer. He offers her living water, saying if she had this water, she would never go thirsty. The woman sarcastically responds, asking where this living water was so she wouldn't have to keep going to the well. Jesus says *he* is the living water. He offers her himself.

At that moment the woman realizes whom she is talking to. Essentially, she asks him if he is the one who had been prophesied, the incarnate God, and Jesus tells her that he is. Taken over by the excitement of her discovery, the woman runs into the town and tells everybody she has met the living God.

There are many things I love about this passage. One of them is that Jesus went to this woman intentionally. In doing so, he revealed our own depravity, because we would be the ones judging him for interacting with such a person.

This same kind of prejudice exists in the church today. Very conservative people will attack you for befriending liberals; those who don't drink will attack you for going into a bar; certain denominations accuse others of not actually being Christians. But Jesus walks right by all of these prejudices and strikes up a vulnerable conversation about the state of our hearts. He is not interested in playing our political games based on prejudice and insecurity.

When we have a relationship with Jesus, we let go of our prejudices. Our identities can no longer come from who likes us and who doesn't or whether we associate with successful, good-looking people or those whom society considers outcasts. Our identity comes from God.

Closing Thoughts

Do you believe God shows no prejudice?

■ Day 4: Jesus Is the Light in Our Darkness

Light and darkness is an ongoing theme in Scripture. We live in darkness, and because of that it is hard for us to see the truth. But let's take a look at what the Bible has to say about it.

Now as Jesus passed by, He saw a man who was blind from birth. And His disciples asked Him, saying, "Rabbi, who sinned, this man or his parents, that he was born blind?"

Jesus answered, "Neither this man nor his parents sinned, but that the works of God should be revealed in him. I must work the works of Him who sent Me while it is day; the night is coming when no one can work. As long as I am in the world, I am the light of the world."

When He had said these things, He spat on the ground and made clay with the saliva; and He anointed the eyes of the blind man with the clay. And He said to him, "Go, wash in the pool of Siloam" (which is translated, Sent). So he went and washed, and came back seeing.

Therefore the neighbors and those who previously had seen that he was blind said, "Is not this he who sat and begged?"

Some said, "This is he." Others said, "He is like him."

He said, "I am he."

Therefore they said to him, "How were your eyes opened?"

He answered and said, "A Man called Jesus made clay and anointed my eyes and said to me, 'Go to the pool of Siloam and wash.' So I went and washed, and I received sight."

Then they said to him, "Where is He?"

He said, "I do not know."

They brought him who formerly was blind to the Pharisees. Now it was a Sabbath when Jesus made the clay and opened his eyes. Then the Pharisees also asked him again how he had received his sight. He said to them, "He put clay on my eyes, and I washed, and I see."

Therefore some of the Pharisees said, "This Man is not from God, because He does not keep the Sabbath."

Others said, "How can a man who is a sinner do such signs?" And there was a division among them.

They said to the blind man again, "What do you say about Him because He opened your eyes?"

He said, "He is a prophet."

But the Jews did not believe concerning him, that he had been blind and received his sight, until they called the parents of him who had received his sight. And they asked them, saying, "Is this your son, who you say was born blind? How then does he now see?"

His parents answered them and said, "We know that this is our son, and that he was born blind; but by what means he now sees we do not know, or who opened his eyes we do not know. He is of age; ask him. He will speak for himself." His parents said these things because they feared the Jews, for the Jews had agreed already that if anyone confessed that He was Christ, he would be put out of the synagogue. Therefore his parents said, "He is of age; ask him."

So they again called the man who was blind, and said to him, "Give God the glory! We know that this Man is a sinner."

He answered and said, "Whether He is a sinner or not I do not know. One thing I know: that though I was blind, now I see."

Then they said to him again, "What did He do to you? How did He open your eyes?"

He answered them, "I told you already, and you did not listen. Why do you want to hear it again? Do you also want to become His disciples?"

Then they reviled him and said, "You are His disciple, but we are Moses' disciples. We know that God spoke to Moses; as for this fellow, we do not know where He is from."

The man answered and said to them, "Why, this is a marvelous thing, that you do not know where He is from; yet He has opened my eyes! Now we know that God does not hear sinners; but if anyone is a worshiper of God and does His will, He hears him. Since the world began it has been unheard of that anyone opened the eyes of one who was born blind. If this Man were not from God, He could do nothing."

They answered and said to him, "You were completely born in sins, and are you teaching us?" And they cast him out.

Jesus heard that they had cast him out; and when He had found him, He said to him, "Do you believe in the Son of God?"

He answered and said, "Who is He, Lord, that I may believe in Him?"

And Jesus said to him, "You have both seen Him and it is He who is talking with you."

Then he said, "Lord, I believe!" And he worshiped Him.

And Jesus said, "For judgment I have come into this world, that those who do not see may see, and that those who see may be made blind."

Then some of the Pharisees who were with Him heard these words, and said to Him, "Are we blind also?"

Jesus said to them, "If you were blind, you would have no sin; but now you say, 'We see.' Therefore your sin remains." (John 9:1–41)

John includes the story of the blind man in his Gospel to illustrate Jesus is God, but also to show us that Jesus has the power to help us see what we were previously unable to see. John shows Jesus healing physical blindness as a *material* example of what he can do for us *spiritually*. This man's blindness was a canvas for Jesus' power. And the greatest miracle wasn't even his physical healing, but the more significant spiritual healing.

Interestingly, Jesus' method of healing this blind man was rather bizarre. Jesus spit in dirt, made some mud, and rubbed it in the man's eyes. He then told him to go and wash the mud away. John recorded no conversation between Jesus and the man. We are given the impression Jesus did this and the man simply obeyed his instructions to wash. The result of his obedience? He came away from the pool with his sight restored. But Jesus wasn't content to leave it at that. He wanted a deeper kind of healing for the man.

As the Pharisees questioned and threatened the blind man, he gradually began to understand the identity of the man who had healed him. Complete understanding comes at the end of the story as Jesus asked him whether or not he believed in the Son of Man, a term commonly used to describe the Messiah. But the man didn't know who Jesus was talking about, so he asked who this Messiah was so that he could believe in him. With no small amount of irony, John tells us Jesus' response: "You have both seen Him and it is He who is talking with you." With this, the man believed and worshiped Jesus.

Jesus wants us to know we need faith. We need to see him with something other than our eyes. It's essential for relationship with Jesus. But we'll never have it unless Jesus brings his light into the darkness of our lives and shows us himself. Jesus can and will heal us of our spiritual blindness so we can see what is really going on in the world and in ourselves. Then we can say along with the man born blind, "One thing I know: that though I was blind, now I see."

Closing Thoughts

Even though you can't physically see Jesus, are you starting to understand the mystery of seeing him?

■ Day 5: What Is This Business of Being Born Again?

One of the goofier-sounding sayings Christians use is that we are "born again." It even feels odd for me to type it. What does it mean to be born again? And where did the saying come from?

The saying actually comes from the Gospel of John. In John 3:1–18, the author tells the story of a religious leader who got curious about this Jesus fellow and went to visit him at night. He went at night because he was a religious leader and if anybody saw him with this controversial figure, Jesus, the man probably would have lost his job. But Nicodemus couldn't help himself. He believed Jesus had authority and, at least to some degree, believed Jesus was telling the truth. And Nicodemus was a seeker of truth. So he went to Jesus and asked how he could have closure in his life, how he could know for sure everything was going to be okay. And that was when Jesus used this peculiar phrase, saying Nicodemus needed to be "born again." Now Nicodemus answered the way you or I might answer: "The idea is absurd; how am I supposed to go back into my mother's womb?"

I love how there was something about Jesus that gave people the freedom to talk openly, even sarcastically with him.

But Jesus saw Nicodemus was seriously missing the point. Jesus told Nicodemus he was talking not about physical birth, but about the kind of spiritual birth that would allow him to enter the kingdom of God. And in explaining how to be reborn spiritually, Jesus said something billions of people have repeated since. It's the most famous verse in the Bible. In John 3:16, Jesus said, "For God so loved the world that He gave His only begotten Son, that whoever believes in Him should not perish but have everlasting life."

However, what is rarely known and only occasionally read is the next statement Jesus made: "For God did not send His Son into the world to condemn the world, but that the world through Him might be saved. He who believes in Him is not condemned; but he who does not believe is condemned already, because he has not believed in the name of the only begotten Son" (vv. 17–18).

There are three very important ideas for Nicodemus (and us) to understand in this verse:

- *God loves the world.* The impact of that thought alone has done more to change human lives than probably any other thought that has entered the mind of man. God does not hate the world; he loves the world.

- *God wants us to trust him.* Like any relationship, our relationship with God is, at its core, a relationship of trust.

- *Jesus did not come to condemn, but to save.* Previously, in our blindness, we thought God came here to judge us and condemn us. But God set Nicodemus straight. God came to save the world. He is not standing in judgment, finding fault with us. He already knows everything that is wrong with us. He doesn't need to condemn us. We do a very good job of that ourselves. He has come to save us because he loves us. He invites us into a relationship with him. And as with all relationships, this one is built on trust.

Later in the Gospel of John, Nicodemus returned. It is a sensational scene, actually, because Nicodemus helped to bury Jesus' body. The reason this scene is so moving is because Nicodemus, a religious leader, was touching the body of a dead man, which was strictly prohibited for a man of his position. In short, he was renouncing all the religious laws and regulations that previously entrapped him. He was proclaiming publicly that he believed Jesus was who he said he was and that he was choosing the person of Jesus over religion.

Closing Thoughts

Are you willing to walk away from everything to follow Jesus, just as Nicodemus did?

Small Group Discussion Questions

These questions will be discussed at your small group meeting.

1. *Have you ever felt like the things you've done would cause God not to like you, not to want a relationship with you?*

How does knowing that Jesus wanted to be friends with Zacchaeus make you feel? (See Day 1.)

2. *Describe a time in your life when you experienced hopelessness.*

Do you think that life is hopeless now, or is there part of you that believes things can be made right and you can experience hope again?

How does Christ fulfilling the hope of the paralyzed man (at the pool at Bethesda) offer hope to your life as well? (See Day 2.)

3. If you could change one thing about yourself, what would it be? Why? (See Day 3.)

4. *Do you believe Jesus accepts you as you are and that your own feelings of insecurity are simply lies?*

Do you want Jesus to help you see everybody as equal, and leave your prejudices and society's contest behind? (See Day 3.)

5. *Have you ever felt blind in life?*

If you have faith in Christ, do you believe he will take away your spiritual blindness and allow you to see?

Will you ask Jesus to heal you of your spiritual blindness? (See Day 4.)

6. *You have now spent three weeks with Christ. You've seen him do miracles and make proclamations, and you've seen some people walk away and others believe. Nicodemus didn't care what anybody else thought. He knew Jesus was the Son of God, and all his hope was in him. As you think about Christ, do you place all your hope in him?*

Can I Know God?

Opening Thoughts

- Do you feel like you fit in the church world? Is that positive, negative, or both?

- What are the messy and broken parts of your life? Do you see redemption there?

- Have you ever been disappointed by the Christian life?

■ Day 1: Who Knows the Father?

When I was a kid, I thought of God as a kind of slot machine in the sky. I'd pray sometimes, but mostly in hopes the cherries would line up and I'd get whatever I was praying for. Essentially, my spirituality looked more like wishful thinking than the relationship talked about in the Bible. In the Bible, people interact with God as though he is a person, as though he has a will and a temper and a heart that can relate to their experiences.

I liked this good-luck/bad-luck system of the slot machine, though. It was convenient. Relationships bring a kind of responsibility that I didn't want. With my version of spirituality, I could do whatever I wanted, and if I got into trouble, I could pray and pull the lever on the slot machine and (perhaps) get out of my predicament.

But one Christmas, as a kid, I woke up in the middle of the night feeling incredibly guilty about not having gotten my mother a present. It was very different from the usual childhood guilt I felt. I realized I had done something wrong—not against

my mom, but against a being whose very essence was love. I knew then that God was real and perfect, and I was real and imperfect. And I saw that the God I had created for myself wasn't God at all.

> No one knows the Son except the Father. Nor does anyone know the Father except the Son, and the one to whom the Son wills to reveal Him. (Matthew 11:27)

In the Bible, Jesus most often talks about our broken relationship with God and what he wants to do to fix that relationship. Jesus' primary concern is whether or not we *know him.*

In Matthew, Jesus says he *knows* the Father. And he says nobody knows the Father except him. I think what Jesus means by this is that for centuries people have been playing a religious guessing game, trying to figure out what version of theology is true. People had worshiped religion rather than God. But Jesus says it's not a knowledge of theology that gets us into heaven; it's knowledge of God. And then Jesus makes a stunning statement: he will introduce us to God. Through Jesus, we can know God. Scripture calls this "reconciliation."

God created man to be in communion with him—that is, to be in relationship with him. But early on, man chose to walk away from God, and that is why things are messed up. If you think about it, it makes a lot of sense. We are very relational beings, and when things are out of whack in our lives, it's usually because something relational isn't going right. The Bible says the relationship between man and God isn't going right, and that is why things are so messed up.

This is the reason Jesus keeps telling us we are in trouble. Ours is a life-threatening, spiritual disease, and we cannot live with this disconnect between us and the author of life. So Jesus came to be among us, to repair this relationship.

Jesus says we can know him, and when we do, we will also know the Father and the Father will know us. But how is knowing Jesus any easier than knowing the Father? Well, we've got four books written specifically about the human life of Jesus (Matthew, Mark, Luke, and John), which helps. For example, listen to what John wrote in his Gospel: "Jesus did many other miraculous signs in the presence of his disciples, which are not recorded in this book. But these are written that you may believe that Jesus is the Christ, the Son of God, and that by believing you may have life in his name" (John 20:30–31 NIV).

The cool thing is that John didn't play the bait-and-switch game. He isn't tricking us into a relationship. He is very clear about what his intentions are. It is as though we're given the chance to have a blind date (platonic, of course) with Jesus. We can get a feel for who he was, and then decide if we want to be in a relationship with him.

All of this sounds very confusing, of course. But think about how confusing your human relationships are. Then try to apply our limited understanding to a relationship with the divine?! Even the apostle Paul said all of this will sound like foolishness to those who have not experienced it (see 1 Corinthians 1:18). But as foolish as it sounds, it is true. God wants us to have a relationship with him. And just as in all relationships, it all starts when something inside us is drawn to another.

The Christian life is us being drawn to the person of Jesus, and eventually coming to believe him, trust him, and follow him. This is the true mark of a Christian: you must *know* Jesus, and through him, God.

Closing Thoughts

What first drew you to Jesus?

■ Day 2: To Know the Father Is Eternal Life

In John 17 we get a remarkable look at a conversation between Jesus and God. Over the course of several years with Jesus, John certainly heard Jesus pray dozens if not hundreds of times. But there was something about this particular prayer that made John want to write it down. Part of the reason, I think, is found in verse 3: "And this is eternal life, that they may know You (the Father), the only true God, and Jesus Christ whom You have sent."

Did you know this is the only place in Scripture where *eternal life* is defined? And what is interesting is that Jesus doesn't describe it in terms of mansions or mountains or streets of gold; he describes it as knowing the Father. Hence, as Jesus has already explained, the way we have eternal life is through a relationship with the Father through Jesus. And that is enough. It is the relationship we've been looking for all our lives.

A small part of us probably wants the mansions and streets of gold, but that is because we don't fully understand the power of relationship. I've been in love before, and when I was in love I didn't dream about a new car or a better house. Back then, all I wanted was to be around her. Although Christian spirituality is not a romantic relationship, it is still a relationship defined by love. And the love we have for God, and his love for us, will trump all other desires. When our relational needs are met, we feel complete and whole. If we truly know Jesus and are in a relationship with him, the streets of gold will pale in comparison to being with him for all of eternity.

Eternity, by definition, lasts forever, but this is something we can't fully comprehend. It is better defined relationally: being completely fulfilled in God, knowing God, and being in relationship with the One from whom all life flows.

As we discussed yesterday, Jesus' purpose on earth was to explain the Father to us, through his words and the way he lived, so we would know him and have a relationship with him through Jesus. He frequently asked people, "Do you believe me? Do you trust me?" because he knew that the heart of every relationship is trust.

Have you felt the strain of broken relationships or experienced a betrayal of trust? You can be assured the ache inside will be fulfilled when you are reunited and reconciled with God through his Son, Jesus. This is the heart of Christian spirituality: to know Jesus, and to know God through Christ.

Closing Thoughts

How would your life change if you truly believed this?

■ Day 3: The Father Longs to Be Known

I used to think of God as this lonely old man with a long gray beard sitting on a throne. Even though he was surrounded by angels, I didn't think they really knew how to relate to him. I mean they sang to him and fanned him with palm leaves and that sort of thing, but it's not like they knocked off after work and got a beer together. But in reality, the God of Scripture isn't this detached at all. He is intensely relational. He loves other people, other beings; they are his children and his creation. He's a doting father, if you will. He is all about relationships. In fact, the God written about in Scripture has never been alone. God has always existed within the context of relationships. He has a relationship with his Son, Jesus, and with the Holy Spirit, and with angels, and yes, even with us. I think you could even say that God basks in relationships.

Jesus expresses this idea in one of his prayers as recorded by John:

> I pray for these followers, but I am also praying for all those who will believe in me because of their teaching. Father, I pray that they can be one. As you are in me and I am in you, I pray that they can also be one in us. Then the world will believe that you sent me. I have given these people the glory that you gave me so that they can be one, just as you and I are one. I will be in them and you will be in me so that they will be completely one. Then the world will know that you sent me and that you loved them just as much as you loved me.
>
> Father, I want these people that you gave me to be with me where I am. I want them to see my glory, which you gave me because you loved me before the world was made. Father, you are the One who is good. The world does not know you, but I know you, and these people know you sent me. I showed them what you are like, and I will show them again. Then they will have the same love that you have for me, and I will live in them. (John 17:20–26 NCV)

God is *in* Jesus and Jesus is *in* God. They are united in mutual love and communion, yet without the loss of personal distinctness. Their relationship is a rich and unclouded fellowship that is so deep and true, so close, and fired by such pure love that Jesus said they are *one*.

Being "one" is a term usually reserved for marriages. But Jesus says very clearly that he and the Father are one, and that he wants you and I to be one with them too. He invites us into this rich, relational community that *is* God. And so, when we know Jesus, we have entered into a relationship with not only him but the Father as well. And the Father loves it. This relationship is better than any relationship we've ever known.

Don't miss this line from Jesus' prayer: "You loved them just as much as you loved me. I showed them what you are like, and I will show them again. Then they will have the same love that you have for me, and I will live in them" (John 17:23, 26 NCV).

These words are so astounding that they border on the unbelievable. Do you hear what Jesus is saying to God? The same love God the Father has for Jesus, God also has for you and me. How can this be? Jesus never failed, yet we sin and fail every day. How could he love us as much as he loves his perfect, divine Son? The reason, of course, is that when we are one with Jesus, we enjoy all the love that Jesus enjoys. The closest metaphor we have to this is that we have *married into the family*.

How much does the Father love the Son? Was there ever a time when he didn't love the Son? Will there ever be a time when he won't love the Son? What does their love look like? Are there personal agendas, petty differences, doubts, and insecurities between the Father and the Son? Can you imagine the Father ever abandoning the Son? When the Father looks at the Son, what do you think he feels?

The answer to all of these questions is that the love the Father has for the Son is perfect. It's such a perfect love that we can't even imagine what it will look like. All human love is beautiful, but it's only beautiful at certain angles, not in its entirety. We are

imperfect, therefore the best of our love is imperfect. But God's love for the Son, and also for us, is perfect indeed.

It bears repeating: the love the Father has for the Son is the same love he has for you and me. God feels toward us exactly as he feels toward his own Son. If this is true, then the Father wants a relationship with you and me as much as he wants a relationship with the Son. Astounding!

What do you think? Can you believe this is true? Consider the words of Jesus: "Father, I want these people that you gave me to be with me where I am. I want them to see my glory" (John 17:24 NCV).

Closing Thoughts

Even if you already knew God loved you, did you realize how much?

■ Day 4: The Father's Heart

Before we start, read the parable of the lost son in Luke 15:11–32.

> Then He said: "A certain man had two sons. And the younger of them said to his father, 'Father, give me the portion of goods that falls to me.' So he divided to them his livelihood. And not many days after, the younger son gathered all together, journeyed to a far country, and there wasted his possessions

with prodigal living. But when he had spent all, there arose a severe famine in that land, and he began to be in want. Then he went and joined himself to a citizen of that country, and he sent him into his fields to feed swine. And he would gladly have filled his stomach with the pods that the swine ate, and no one gave him anything.

"But when he came to himself, he said, 'How many of my father's hired servants have bread enough and to spare, and I perish with hunger! I will arise and go to my father, and will say to him, "Father, I have sinned against heaven and before you, and I am no longer worthy to be called your son. Make me like one of your hired servants."'

"And he arose and came to his father. But when he was still a great way off, his father saw him and had compassion, and ran and fell on his neck and kissed him. And the son said to him, 'Father, I have sinned against heaven and in your sight, and am no longer worthy to be called your son.'

"But the father said to his servants, 'Bring out the best robe and put it on him, and put a ring on his hand and sandals on his feet. And bring the fatted calf here and kill it, and let us eat and be merry; for this my son was dead and is alive again; he was lost and is found.' And they began to be merry.

"Now his older son was in the field. And as he came and drew near to the house, he heard music and dancing. So he called one of the servants and asked what these things meant. And he said to him, 'Your brother has come, and because he has received him safe and sound, your father has killed the fatted calf.'

"But he was angry and would not go in. Therefore his father came out and pleaded with him. So he answered and said to his father, 'Lo, these many years I have been serving you; I never transgressed your commandment at any time; and yet you never gave me a young goat, that I might make merry with my friends. But as soon as this son of yours came, who has devoured your livelihood with harlots, you killed the fatted calf for him.'

"And he said to him, 'Son, you are always with me, and all that I have is yours. It was right that we should make merry and be glad, for your brother was dead and is alive again, and was lost and is found.'"

Now, let me modernize this story a bit:

If updated to fit today's culture, the parable of the prodigal son might look more like a young twentysomething taking his early inheritance from the family construction company and going off to Vegas to waste it all on blackjack, prostitutes, drugs, and expensive hotel rooms. Jesus isn't afraid to paint the story pretty dark. This kid is as irresponsible as they come. But back home, the kid's father never gets bitter; he never takes it personally. He can't force his son to come home—that wouldn't allow him his autonomy—but still he hopes his son will return. And Jesus wants us to know that the father hoped his son would return because the father *loved* the son. There really was no other motive.

As the modern version of the story might go, the kid loses everything back in Vegas. He ends up owing a casino a bunch of cash and has to clean toilets to pay his debts. He has to sleep on the street and eat other people's leftovers out of trash cans. Pretty soon, the kid realizes he'd be eating a lot better if he were back home with his father.

So he comes to his senses and realizes his foolishness. In his heart he knows he has sinned against heaven and his father. Broken and humbled, he decides to go home and ask his dad to forgive him.

This is the story Jesus is telling. But the point isn't that we must repent and run home. (At least that isn't the main point.) What Jesus wants us to understand is the father's patient and unconditional love for his son.

Jesus says this: "When he was still a long way off, his father saw him. His heart pounding, he ran out, embraced him, and kissed him" (Luke 15:20 MSG).

Instead of being indignant with his son and heaping guilt on him, the father welcomes him home with an enormous, costly celebration. The father says: "My son was dead and is alive again" (Luke 15:24).

This is a really different picture of God than a lot of people probably have. Honestly, it's a different picture of God than I have. Every time I read this story I am reminded that God isn't a bitter old man shaking his finger at me, making me feel dirty and wrong. It's almost hard to believe, but if what Jesus is saying is true, then God throws a party for us when we come home, no matter what we've done while we're away.

Some may say the father threw a party because the son admitted his failure and foolishness. But Luke is very careful with Jesus' words here. When the father *saw* his son, he was *filled with compassion* for him. Before the father heard one word of confession from his son, he *ran* to him and *threw his arms around him* and *kissed* him. The father's compassion and love was not contingent on whether or not his son confessed. This is a love unlike anything we know of human relationships. The love our heavenly Father has for his children causes him to throw a party when we return from trying to go through life without him. And it doesn't matter how bad we were; it only matters that we have decided to come home.

No matter where we've been or how long we've been there, no matter what unspeakable things we've done, no matter how ashamed we are of ourselves, the Father's heart is filled with compassion toward us.

Closing Thoughts

Are you willing to return the Father's embrace?

■ Day 5: The Open Invitation

> Come to Me, all you who labor and are heavy laden, and I will give you rest. Take My yoke upon you and learn from Me, for I am gentle and lowly in heart, and you will find rest for your souls. For My yoke is easy and My burden is light. (Matthew 11:28–30)

I was listening to the radio in my car the other day and heard Sting singing, "If you love somebody, set them free." I've been thinking so much about relationships as I write this book, and the lyrics made a lot of sense to me. Have you ever been in a relationship with somebody who has a really bad temper? If so, you were probably in a relationship with somebody who was afraid you'd leave them. That's why people get angry, because anger is one way we control others. But God, our passionate Father, isn't controlling. He doesn't force us to love him. Forced love has no authenticity. It is only reactionary, a fear-based emotion. It's a very unfulfilling way to live, and it will never create a successful relationship. Sting isn't exactly a great theologian of our time, but his song succinctly captures the way God relates to us: he sets us free but *invites* us into a relationship with him.

There are certain assertions embedded in this invitation, however. Jesus knows we will not thrive, or even survive, without the love of God. He also knows our sinful nature will not be able to mingle with God and that we need to be one with him in order to be reconciled to the Father. And so this isn't your run-of-the-mill invitation into a relationship. There are consequences for saying no. Jesus is inviting us into the most blessed relationship we can possibly imagine, but because we cannot live without God, he also wants us to know we will surely die if we don't accept this love. He isn't saying this to be controlling. He is saying this because the nature of God is so good that nothing can even be good, or even be truly alive, outside of a relationship with him.

In fact, Jesus sees how very hard we are working as a result of our relationship with God being broken. He sees us trying to get people to like us, trying to get people to say we are good-looking or hard workers or that we matter in our company or in our families or our society. He saw us back when we were children, when we wanted our parents to notice us; he sees us now that we are adults, trying so hard to succeed so people will think we are important, trying to lose weight so people won't look down on us for being out of shape. Jesus sees us and says, "Your burden is too much; your workload is too heavy." Then he invites us to exchange our burden for his, which is much easier to carry. Jesus has a relationship with the Father, and there isn't a moment in all of Scripture in which he is wondering whether or not he matters, whether or not anybody loves him. He is confident in the love of the Father, and he invites us into that wonderful love too.

A lot of us fear a relationship with God because we are afraid he is going to be like our parents or like our spouse or like our bosses. But God is not like any human we know. He has no sin nature and he loves perfectly. He is not an aggressive, morally superior tyrant whose power is out of control. His strength is very much under control. He is gentle. He is humble.

Just like the father in Jesus' story of the prodigal son that we looked at yesterday, God scans the horizon waiting patiently for us to come home to him. He is the Father who sees us a long way off. And filled with the same compassion for us as he has for the Son, *he runs to us* and throws his arms around us.

This is the God that Jesus invites us to know.

This is God, whom we have been longing for all our lives.

Closing Thoughts

How has God revealed his character to you? (What characteristics of his have you seen most clearly?)

Small Group Discussion Questions

These questions will be discussed at your small group meeting.

1. *As you read stories about Jesus, do you feel yourself being drawn to him?*

Does part of you want to get to know him better?

What do you think of the idea that God wants to know you? (See Day 1.)

2. *When you look around, do you see that much of the pain in your life comes out of relationships? (See Day 2.)*

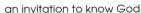

3. *How does it make you feel to know God will fulfill all that you are missing through a relationship with him, and that this relationship will last forever? (See Day 2.)*

4. *How does it make you feel to know that God wants a relationship with you?*

How does it make you feel to know God's love is completely perfect? (See Day 3.)

5. *How does it feel to know that no matter what you have done—whether you have committed a crime, lied to a friend, cheated on a spouse, or shaken your fist at God— God will throw a party for you when you return?*

Is this something you believe about God? (See Day 4.)

6. How hard have you worked to get people to notice you?

Have you caught yourself wondering, If I were only more successful, more thin, or more talented, my life would be better? (See Day 5.)

100

7. *What would it look like for you to come home?*

If you haven't yet, pray and take God up on his invitation. Tell him you'd like to know him and be in a relationship with him. The God of the Bible will run and meet you in that place. (See Day 5.)

How Do We Follow Jesus?

Opening Thoughts

- Do you feel that your significance in life is your own responsibility?

- Is there anything you'd be willing to give up your life for?

- Has faith met any needs in your life in a real way (i.e., emotionally, practically, etc.)?

■ Day 1: Why Did Jesus Have to Die?

Becoming a Christian doesn't mean you have to become religious or vote a certain way or adhere to any other stereotype associated with religious people. Becoming a Christian simply means you have entered into a relationship with Jesus Christ.

And so in asking the question "What does it mean to live as a Christian?" we really have to ask, "What does it mean to know and follow Jesus? What does it look like to be in a relationship with Jesus? And how does it grow?"

Just as friendships with other people grow and get stronger with time and experience, so does our relationship with Jesus. We spend time with him by praying and talking to him, and by reading the Bible and continuing to meditate and study the Book that first introduced us to him. We also grow when we spend time with others who know him, sharing stories and experiences with them.

The important thing to remember in all this is that Christianity is not about right and wrong any more than marriage is about

right and wrong. While rules are part of any relationship, very few people would define their marriage in those terms. Rather, they would describe their relationship through experiences and stories. It's no different with Christ.

But let me backtrack for a minute and talk about a unique aspect of our relationship with Jesus. When I first saw Steven Spielberg's film *Saving Private Ryan*, I thought, *Why did Tom Hanks have to die?* I liked him. And I remember feeling the same way when I first read John's Gospel. I remember liking Jesus, and when the soldiers started to kill him, I actually set the Bible down and didn't want to read any more. You can say a lot about Jesus, even that he was not the Son of God, but it's hard to say he was a bad man, and it's hard to argue he deserved to die. He didn't.

The funny thing is, Jesus never saw his life this way. Jesus came *to die*. That was the point of his life on earth. He even called the time of his death "his hour."

Read John 12:23–33:

Jesus answered them, saying, "The hour has come that the Son of Man should be glorified. Most assuredly, I say to you, unless a grain of wheat falls into the ground and dies, it remains alone; but if it dies, it produces much grain. He who loves his life will lose it, and he who hates his life in this world will keep it for eternal life. If anyone serves Me, let him follow Me; and where I am, there My servant will be also. If anyone serves Me, him My Father will honor.

"Now My soul is troubled, and what shall I say? 'Father, save Me from this hour'? But for this purpose I came to this hour. Father, glorify Your name."

Then a voice came from heaven, saying, "I have both glorified it and will glorify it again."

Therefore the people who stood by and heard it said that it had thundered. Others said, "An angel has spoken to Him."

Jesus answered and said, "This voice did not come because of Me, but for your sake. Now is the judgment of this world; now the ruler of this world will be cast out. And I, if I am lifted up from the earth, will draw all peoples to Myself." This He said, signifying by what death He would die.

Unlike many heroes who die in stories, Jesus' death was not tragic. His life was not taken from him. The biblical writers are very clear to point out that Jesus *gave* his life, that he "laid it down." He didn't have to. It was a voluntary choice on his part (see John 10:14–18).

While Jesus was hanging on the cross, he was mocked by people who looked on. Anybody who would choose to entertain themselves by watching an execution is a rough character already, but to mock a dying man would mean Jesus was surrounded by some of the worst kinds of people in the community. They sarcastically called to him, "Save Yourself, and come down from the cross" (Mark 15:30). When I read that, I wondered why he didn't. If he was the Son of God, he certainly could have. He could have shown them exactly who he was and whipped some serious tail. But he didn't. He chose not to.

Why?

According to Scripture, Jesus died to reconcile broken humanity to his Father. The relationship between us and God was destroyed when *we* walked away from *him*. It's important to note that God did not walk away. God is not the reason life is broken. Life is broken because we are broken. In fact, we are more than broken. We are dying, both physically and spiritually. The apostle Paul put it this way: "The wages of sin is death" (Romans 6:23).

Someone had to pay a price for our sin, and this price was death. Jesus chose to pay the penalty, and he died. And because of Jesus' death on the cross, we owe nothing.

Many people fear religion because they think it is manipulative, that religion will steal their freedom. Now to be sure, Christianity espouses a moral ethic, but at the core Christianity is more than just morality. At the very basic level,

at the level of sin and consequence, Christianity espouses something very different: grace. By *grace* I mean a complete forgiveness of sin, no penalty whatsoever. No death. The price has been paid in full. And because of Jesus' sacrifice, we are free to be made one, in perfect unity, with him.

Closing Thoughts

Why would Jesus care for us so much to do this?

■ Day 2: Steps in the Right Direction

What kind of relationship do we have with Jesus when we become a Christian? The Bible says we are "betrothed," and there will be a spiritual wedding in heaven, a great celebration. There are many metaphors for our relationship with the Father, but the metaphor of bride to bridegroom is fitting because Jesus invites us into oneness with him. Our entire identity is wrapped up in Jesus. For now, though, we are still on earth, still dealing with our flesh and many of the problems it creates. Our salvation is set aside and guaranteed. We have been bought with a price. But in a way, we are kind of like that couple who is engaged but still lives separately. So for now our new faith is just about being in relationship with God, getting to know him.

In any relationship, the most important aspect is trust. In biblical terms, this is called "faith."

5

Now after the two days He departed from there and went to Galilee. For Jesus Himself testified that a prophet has no honor in his own country. So when He came to Galilee, the Galileans received Him, having seen all the things He did in Jerusalem at the feast; for they also had gone to the feast.

So Jesus came again to Cana of Galilee where He had made the water wine. And there was a certain nobleman whose son was sick at Capernaum. When he heard that Jesus had come out of Judea into Galilee, he went to Him and implored Him to come down and heal his son, for he was at the point of death. Then Jesus said to him, "Unless you people see signs and wonders, you will by no means believe."

The nobleman said to Him, "Sir, come down before my child dies!"

Jesus said to him, "Go your way; your son lives." So the man believed the word that Jesus spoke to him, and he went his way. And as he was now going down, his servants met him and told him, saying, "Your son lives!"

Then he inquired of them the hour when he got better. And they said to him, "Yesterday at the seventh hour the fever left him." So the father knew that it was at the same hour in which Jesus said to him, "Your son lives." And he himself believed, and his whole household. (John 4:43–53)

This is the story of a man who traveled two days to see Jesus. He was a powerful man, but his son was sick, and even though he had lots of money and was a respected authority in his city, there was nothing he could do to heal his son. So he went to Jesus.

When Jesus said, "Go your way; your son lives" (John 4:50), the man didn't beg him to come back to his home, and he didn't ask for assurance that his son had been healed. Instead, John wrote, "The man believed the word that Jesus spoke to him, and he went his way" (v. 50).

The man had faith, and throughout Scripture, faith and trust are praised while doubt is warned against. As we begin our

relationship with Jesus, the first thing we need to understand, then, is that he wants us to have faith.

Here is the great thing: Jesus' motive for wanting us to have faith is not so he can take advantage of us. Remember, he died for us; he has proven his love. No, Jesus wants us to have faith because he is trustworthy and faithful.

But here is another thing you will experience when entering into a relationship with Jesus: Your faith will grow. Your faith will get stronger.

In the story John told, the man was walking home and his servants came out to meet him to tell him his son was well. John tells us that the official inquired as to when his child got better. Listen to John's words: "So the father knew that it was at the same hour in which Jesus said to him, 'Your son lives.' And he himself believed, and his whole household" (John 4:53).

Hadn't this man already believed? Yes, he took Jesus at his word. But John makes a point to teach us something about the nature of faith: it will grow.

When you accept Christ's invitation to walk through life with him, it's not a static decision. It's stepping into a lifestyle of trusting him every day. Faith is dynamic; it is a living, growing, and vital part of our relationship with God.

Closing Thoughts

Reflect on a relationship you've had (with God or another human) that continually exercised and proved its trust.

■ Day 3: The Greatest Thing

Jesus didn't mix well with the religious leaders of his day. He understood the heart of man and knew man was easily corrupted by power and greed. Often the people who claimed to represent God were the people he had the most problems with. Jesus didn't think religious people were any less corrupt than criminals or tax collectors. He saw everybody the same—completely broken.

Justice and love are the first things to disappear when power and greed corrupt the hearts of man. In fact, when Jesus rebuked the religious leaders, he said precisely that they "neglect justice and the love of God" (Luke 11:42 NIV).

When the Bible talks about our brokenness, it is referring to a lack of love. We are separated from the love of God and so we have no access to true love. Oh, sure, we can love people, but the kind of love Jesus is talking about is perfect love, the love that only comes from God.

When John records for us Jesus' last conversation with his best friends, the statement Jesus repeats most often is, "Love one another as I have loved you." Jesus says this at least six times in John 13—16. Now imagine having dinner with somebody and

listening to them repeat the same phrase over and over. This was obviously very important to Jesus. He even took it a step further by saying, "By this all men will know that you are my disciples, if you love one another" (John 13:35 NIV). In other words, the manner in which we conduct our lives will be so marked by authentic love for others that people will notice and wonder why, and they will soon realize we are followers of Jesus.

The Bible says we follow Jesus by obeying him, and the first thing he wants us to do is love one another. When asked what is the greatest commandment in the Torah (the first five books of the Old Testament), Jesus said: "You shall love the LORD your God with all your heart, with all your soul, and with all your strength" (Deuteronomy 6:5). And the second greatest commandment is similar: "Love your neighbor as yourself" (Leviticus 19:18). Then Jesus commented on the importance of these two statements. He said, "On these two commandments hang all the Law and the Prophets" (Matthew 22:40). Essentially, what Jesus was saying is that the entire Hebrew Bible, known as the Old Testament, is summarized and built on these two ideas. Jesus was saying this: the point is love.

Closing Thoughts

God's entire agenda is to love us. As you follow him, how will you love others?

■ Day 4: What Do We Build Our Lives On?

The most famous of all Jesus' recorded speeches or sermons is called the Sermon on the Mount. The longest and most complete version is found in Matthew 5—7. You may be wondering, *As a follower of Jesus, how do I live?* Jesus answers much of that question in this sermon, and he closes by saying that if we obey him, we will be like a person who has built his house on the rock.

> Therefore whoever hears these sayings of Mine, and does them, I will liken him to a wise man who built his house on the rock: and the rain descended, the floods came, and the winds blew and beat on that house; and it did not fall, for it was founded on the rock. (Matthew 7:24–25)

What is this rock? It is the principles in this sermon and the rest of the Bible. I used to not like the Bible because I thought it was boring. But when I take the approach that reading the Bible is spending time with Jesus, who loves me more than any human could, it makes me feel differently about it. The bottom line is that we get to know Jesus by spending time reading the Bible.

To use a metaphor the Bible itself uses, the Scriptures are not unlike food. We need the Scriptures for our spiritual growth and health. They are our primary source for knowing God. Only in the Scriptures has God specifically revealed who he is and what he is like.

Jesus said, "If you love Me, keep My commandments" (John 14:15). Following Jesus means obeying him, and his instructions are found in the Bible.

I am not saying the Bible is a magic book that has instruction for every situation we may encounter. Rather, God's words become the lens through which we understand life as he intended. What God offers us in the Bible is perspective and

wisdom, and with that perspective and wisdom we have all the tools we need to make good decisions.

So if I want to know God and follow the Jesus I've encountered, then I need to spend time reading God's Word. It reveals the mind and heart of God. And as one who wants to follow him, I want to think and feel as he does. Knowing God gives me a perspective on life that is larger, more encompassing, and, many would say, wise. The Bible says it best: "Your word is a lamp to my feet and a light to my path" (Psalm 119:105).

Closing Thoughts

Do you read the Bible as often as you'd like to?

■ Day 5: Following Jesus' Example

Now before the Feast of the Passover, when Jesus knew that His hour had come that He should depart from this world to the Father, having loved His own who were in the world, He loved them to the end.

And supper being ended, the devil having already put it into the heart of Judas Iscariot, Simon's son, to betray Him, Jesus, knowing that the Father had given all things into His hands, and that He had come from God and was going to God, rose from supper and laid aside His garments, took a towel and girded Himself. After that, He poured water into a

basin and began to wash the disciples' feet, and to wipe them with the towel with which He was girded. Then He came to Simon Peter. And Peter said to Him, "Lord, are You washing my feet?"

Jesus answered and said to him, "What I am doing you do not understand now, but you will know after this."

Peter said to Him, "You shall never wash my feet!"

Jesus answered him, "If I do not wash you, you have no part with Me."

Simon Peter said to Him, "Lord, not my feet only, but also my hands and my head!"

Jesus said to him, "He who is bathed needs only to wash his feet, but is completely clean; and you are clean, but not all of you." For He knew who would betray Him; therefore He said, "You are not all clean."

So when He had washed their feet, taken His garments, and sat down again, He said to them, "Do you know what I have done to you? You call Me Teacher and Lord, and you say well, for so I am. If I then, your Lord and Teacher, have washed your feet, you also ought to wash one another's feet. For I have given you an example, that you should do as I have done to you. Most assuredly, I say to you, a servant is not greater than his master; nor is he who is sent greater than he who sent him. If you know these things, blessed are you if you do them. (John 13:1–17)

In this passage, Jesus was having a final dinner conversation with his closest friends. But before John tells us what Jesus said, he gives us the backdrop for the conversation. It was the night before Passover. Women and children were hurrying around town, getting those last-minute things they needed for the most significant family meal of the year. There was a spirit of mystery and thoughts of the sacred among all the Jews they passed on the street. The comfort that surrounds tradition and holidays settled among the friends as they looked for a place to celebrate their Passover dinner.

But Jesus had one last thing in mind, one last lesson for his friends. They were likely expecting deep theological teaching, but instead Jesus performed a task reserved for the servants of a household: he washed their feet. Now in those days servants washed their masters' feet because their sandaled feet became easily dirty on dirt roads. Washing somebody's feet was never something *important* people did. It was a peasant's role. But through this incredible act of authentic humility, Jesus was teaching his friends that God wants to serve them just as he wants them to serve others.

When Jesus finished he said, "If I then, your Lord and Teacher, have washed your feet, you also ought to wash one another's feet. For I have given you an example, that you should do as I have done to you" (John 13:14–15).

Jesus called upon his followers to treat each other with humility. In one swoop, Jesus dissolves the game we play when we try to decide who is better among us. If God would wash our feet, then who are we to think we are above the task, or for that matter, above anybody else?

The real joy of the Christian life is that we get to stop playing the game of who is better than whom. If I am honest with myself, and I mean really honest, I realize that most of the things I do are in order to feel important. Sadly, I write books, in part, because it makes me feel important, like I am contributing something to society. I buy the clothes I wear because they make me look better, which is not something easy to do. My need for acceptance, to feel important and valued, is embedded in nearly every motive I have. And when Jesus knelt down to wash his friends' feet, he was essentially saying that we don't have to play those games any longer. In fact, we are free. We are as loved scrubbing toilets as we would be if we were kings. We are truly free to serve and love people, without manipulation or requirements of anything in return.

What would it look like if a community of people lived like this?

- No one would do things to fulfill selfish ambitions.

- All people would be treated with dignity and respect.

- Preference would be shown for the needs of others.

- Forgiveness, grace, and mercy would thrive, and justice would prevail.

A life in Jesus is a life completely and totally free. We no longer have to worry about whether or not we will be loved, and we no longer have to do crazy things to win the love of others. In fact, we are finally free to actually love other people for real, without manipulating them into loving us back. When we are in Christ, we have the relationship for which we were designed—a relationship with God. This is our hope, and as the apostle Paul said, it is a hope that will not disappoint (see Romans 5:5).

Closing Thoughts

How has God's love changed your life?

 an invitation to know God

Small Group Discussion Questions

These questions will be discussed at your small group meeting.

1. *Have you ever wondered if there was a secret penalty for being yourself? I don't mean for the small things you do, like telling white lies or passing petty judgment, but a penalty for the person you are. How do you feel about the fact that Jesus has completely paid that penalty? (See Day 1.)*

2. *What does a relationship look like when there is no trust?*

116

What does it look like to trust Jesus?

How can we grow in trust with Jesus? (See Day 2.)

3. In your life, who has withheld love from you? Can you forgive them?

From whom have you withheld love? Why? (See Day 3.)

4. *Upon what are you building your life? Are you willing to let Scripture be your daily food?*

Write out your goals for yourself that you would like to put into practice daily. (See Day 4.)

5. *Where will you go from here? How will you plan to live differently now? What will change in your life? (See Day 5.)*

"I never liked jazz music because jazz music doesn't resolve. . . . I used to not like God because God didn't resolve. But that was before any of this happened."

In Donald Miller's early years, he was vaguely familiar with a distant God. But when he came to know Jesus Christ, he pursued the Christian life with great zeal. Within a few years he had a successful ministry that ultimately left him feeling empty, burned out, and, once again, far away from God. In this intimate, soul-searching account, Miller describes his remarkable journey back to a culturally relevant, infinitely loving God.

Jazz Notes is the literary equivalent of a remix CD

Cool sound-bytes strategically crafted from Don Miller's classic *Blue Like Jazz*, combined with brand new material that offers the author's fans an inside look at some of the unforgettable—and outrageous—characters and stories from the original best seller.

Jazz Notes includes a bonus audio CD with Don Miller interview.

This classic road trip will inspire readers of all ages.

Don Miller recounts his trip with wide-eyed honesty in achingly beautiful prose, discussing everything from the nature of friendship, the reason for pain, and the origins of beauty. As Don and Paul travel from Texas to Oregon in Paul's cantankerous Volkswagen van, the two friends encounter a variety of fascinating people, witness the fullness of nature's splendor, and learn unexpected lessons about themselves, each other, and even God.